TRUSSED UP

How the Daily Mail tied itself in knots over the Tory leadership

Liz Gerard

Cover – Dean Stockton

Published by Bite-Sized Books Ltd 2022

Bite-Sized Books Ltd 8th Floor, 20 St. Andrews Street, London EC4A 3AY, UK

Registered in the UK. Company Registration

No: 9395379

ISBN: 978-1-7391524-9-9

The Daily Mail is Britain's best-selling newspaper. This is a study of its coverage of the Conservative party leadership and government policies from the day Boris Johnson left office in July 2022 until the day Rishi Sunak became prime minister the following October.

Pages from the Mail, published by DMG Media Limited, and other newspapers are reproduced to show the context, projection and direction of the paper's news and opinion pieces over that time. Under the principle of fair dealing, we have reproduced no more than necessary. The articles contained within these pages are not intended to be readable. We acknowledge the publishers' ownership of the typographical arrangement of these pages, which have been collated through the NLA Media Access newspaper library.

Readers who wish to read the articles examined in this study are advised to visit **Dailymail.co.uk**.

Contents

Acknowledgements

Thanks are due to James Evelegh of In Publishing for inspiring this enterprise and to publishers Paul Davies and Julian Costley for having faith in the project.

I am grateful, too, to those who supported the nascent SubScribe blog and convinced me there was a life beyond Wapping. They include, but are not restricted to, Martin Barrow, Roy Greenslade, Matt Kelly, Dominic Ponsford, Michael Prowse and Enid Shelmerdine.

Sub-editors are too often dismissed as drones who slash and mangle 'real' journalists' prose. They aren't. Graham Greene and Bill Bryson were/are exceptional in their talent, but not in the fact of their having been Times subs with something of their own to say. There are hundreds of others on newspapers across the land who also have more to them than the diligence to check a name in Who's Who or the wit to turn a slick headline. Subduing their own voices at work, they save reporters from themselves day in, day out, yet are rewarded more often than not with approbation for the errors that do get through, while the rescue missions go unnoticed or unremarked. I salute this underappreciated army in which I once served.

Special thanks are due to another veteran of that army, who prefers to remain incognito. For his editorial wisdom and encouragement – and for the friendship, bordering on insanity, that led him to read this lot in the middle of a freezing, starless night in Kielder Forest. What a birthday treat!

Liz Gerard

Liz Gerard worked in newspapers for more than 40 years, 30 of them at The Times, where she was one of the night editors. She now speaks and writes about print journalism, having set up the award-winning SubScribe blog in 2012. She has been a judge for the British Journalism Awards since their inception a decade ago and tweets prolifically about the media and politics as @gameoldgirl.

She lives with her family in rural Essex, where she struggles with an overgrown garden and an unruly springer spaniel.

She wishes she were thin, that she had a cat, and that the Daily Mail would be a little gentler.

Introduction

> *'Blessed with Yorkshire grit, Miss Truss has the boldness, imagination and strength of conviction to build on what Boris began.'*

So opined the Daily Mail on August 3, in a full-page editorial endorsement as Conservative party members started voting for our new prime minister.

Eleven weeks on, its leader writers gathered a different clutch of adjectives from their colourful lexicon to describe the same woman: 'hopelessly out of her depth'; a 'lethal combination of incompetence, unforced errors, self-delusion, untethered ambition and hubris'. She had turned the party of Churchill and Thatcher into a laughing stock.

The Tory membership had taken the Mail's advice and installed Liz Truss in Downing Street. But just six weeks after celebrating her success with an 'historic special edition', the Mail was heralding another 'new dawn for Britain' as Rishi Sunak moved into No 10.

It was quite the journey. One that had started when Boris Johnson was forced out at the beginning of the summer. 'What the hell have they done?' the Mail thundered back then, when it had no doubt that Sunak was the villain of the piece. For it was his resignation that had removed the bung from the dyke and brought the deluge that swept Johnson out of office.

It mattered not that Johnson was ousted on a matter of integrity; because his ministers were not prepared to carry on lying for him. For the Mail – which disliked his 'race' to net zero, his green taxes, his lockdown strategy, his social care levy, his borrowing and his spending – he was a winner with a huge public mandate and that was what counted. Everyone knew his faults, but these should be overlooked in the interests of the bigger picture.

He had been the victim of an outbreak of collective hysteria among Tory MPs, driven by enemies (the Left, embittered Remainers, the BBC, the wokerati) who had concocted a mountain out of a molehill of trivial misdemeanours. Trivialities such as the lockdown drinking culture in

Downing Street (including a raucous party on the night before the Duke of Edinburgh's funeral), which is now written off by the Mail as 'a birthday cake that never came out of its Tupperware box'.

(All of this is still the subject of a parliamentary standards inquiry, which the Mail describes as a witch-hunt, a kangaroo court that should be disbanded because its verdict is a foregone conclusion that cannot help but be tainted.)

Now he had been dethroned, defenestrated, brought down in a moment of regicidal lunacy by political pygmies who had more weapons than the killers on the Orient Express: knives, blades, daggers, swords, rapiers, stilettos and axes were all 'plunged' into the great man's back. He was even served hemlock.

Still, what was done was done and, with the occasional wistful backward glance, the paper set about making sure it got the person it wanted in Downing Street. And that person was Liz Truss.

Johnson's resignation and his period as 'caretaker' prime minister, unwilling to hand over to anyone else or to do anything (other than go on holiday) that might tie the hands of his successor, left the country in a state of suspended animation for the whole summer, with no effective government as economic storms built up.

It took the Conservative party two months to choose Johnson's successor. This did not trouble the Mail at first. It said members should take their time because they would have only one shot at finding the right person. It took the Mail two days.

While counselling 'don't rush', it was also urging MPs to 'coalesce' – a word it would use a lot in the ensuing months – around a 'unity' figure from the Right to make sure members had a 'real choice' in the final run-off ballot between the MPs' top two candidates. In other words, find someone who could beat Sunak.

At the time, the Conservatives were some ten points behind Labour in the polls. The Mail was convinced that Labour could never win an overall majority, but it feared that Sir Keir Starmer could 'cobble together' a 'coalition of chaos' with the SNP, Liberal Democrats and the Greens that might keep the Tories out of office forever. By the time Truss resigned after just 44 days as premier, Labour was 37 points ahead and in a position to wipe out the Conservatives with no need for coalitions or apparent risk of having to run a minority administration.

Over the course of that leadership campaign, the Mail promoted and projected Truss as a strong leader-in-waiting, just as it had done with 'strong and stable, crush the saboteurs' Theresa May during the Brexit traumas of the last decade. It mustered all the might of its often vitriol-dipped pen to secure Truss's election, exaggerating her qualifications for the job way beyond anything discernible to the casual onlooker – had it never seen the cheese and pork market videos? – and rubbishing her biggest rivals.

First it set out to destroy the main threat to her place on the final ballot paper – Penny Mordaunt – and then to denigrate Sunak (although it was punctilious in crediting him for measures he took to keep businesses afloat during the pandemic – after all, he might win and the Mail would then have to sell him to the country).

In truth, the Mail had never been a big fan of Sunak, particularly after his National Insurance increase, which was introduced (though the paper tends not to mention this) to fulfil Johnson's ambition to 'fix social care'.

It didn't think the public were big fans either. And the overriding priority of its coverage of the Tory party shenanigans was electability. Leading articles invoked 'struggling families', but people were more often described as 'voters', with concern about them more focused on how they might punish the Tories at the ballot box than on how policies were affecting their lives. The greatest fear was that the Conservatives would be 'consigned to oblivion', of Starmer the socialist being allowed anywhere near power. And so Tory MPs were hectored about the importance of unity and of getting behind their leader.

The 'Left' (which later metamorphosed into Truss's 'anti-growth coalition') had grown into a monstrous threat that included not only the official Opposition, Nicola Sturgeon, the Civil Service and the BBC, but half the Tory party as well. The appointment of Jeremy Hunt and Grant Shapps to replace Kwasi Kwarteng and Suella Braverman after the mini-Budget imploded was a 'liberal left coup'. Sunak, a committed Brexiteer who is happy to send asylum-seekers to Rwanda, was not rightwing enough for Ted Verity and Paul Dacre.

To keep Sunak out of No 10, they did all they could to portray Liz Truss as the country's saviour. She was given three guest columns and two interviews, all of which produced lead stories for the paper. Sunak had the one – at the bottom of an inside spread, with no signposting from the front.

From the day Boris Johnson resigned to the day Rishi Sunak took office – a total of 90 issues, including 10 virtually politics-free days after the death of the Queen – the paper ran more than 60 leading articles devoted to the Tory leadership and Truss's fiscal event. Six – including the one that opens this piece – occupied an entire page. The Mail is wont to chide 'recalcitrant' MPs for their self-importance, but is not shy with regard to its own authority to tell politicians how to run the country.

These leaders had five core themes: Boris is wonderful and was shamefully betrayed, Liz is the next best thing, the mini-Budget is brilliant, Tories must unite or face the catastrophe of Starmer in Downing Street and, finally, the conversion to Rishi.

Then there was the news coverage: 45 front-page leads, 300 inside news pages, plus 60 bylined opinion pieces.

When Truss was declared the winner, the paper was delighted – 'Cometh the hour, cometh the woman' – and predicted in a leader 'the Tory fightback starts today'. It was even more delighted when she wasted no time in getting her friend Kwasi Kwarteng to announce the tax cuts she had promised throughout the campaign – the ones Sunak had repeatedly denounced as fairy tale economics. The Mail message all along had been that Sunak was wrong and she was right. When the 'fiscal event' took place – so called because it obviated the need for any independent outside scrutiny – the paper's splash was 'At last! A true Tory budget'.

Trussonomics was going to cast aside the 'grinding Treasury orthodoxy', turbocharge growth and jolt the economy out of the doldrums after two decades of stagnation. (The Conservatives had been in power for 12 of those years; the Mail was still mourning the ousting of Boris Johnson and seething over the precipitative resignation of Sunak, the most recent guardians of that sclerotic, sluggish, struggling, stagnating economy. If the paper had had its way, they would still be running it.)

When the sky fell in, the Mail – which prizes loyalty above almost any other quality – stuck with Truss through thin and thinner. She had been right, the markets were rabidly over-reacting. The Bank of England was to blame, City slickers were to blame, the IMF was to blame, Putin was to blame.

Again, the editorials focused on the need for unity, on Tory MPs' 'duty' to get behind the prime minister. Many pints were drunk in many last-chance saloons, 'witless' MPs were Gadarene swine or turkeys voting for Christmas, peeling the spuds and putting themselves in the oven.

One by one, columnists from Andrew Neil and Sarah Vine to Stephen Glover and Richard Littlejohn, expressed growing qualms about Truss. But only in her administration's death throes did the paper itself criticise her, and then for her bungled presentation, not her policies. Only at the bitter end did it desert her.

It's hard to fault the Mail on grounds of consistency over this period. It had said time and again that the Tories must unite behind their chosen leader because it was imperative that the party should win the next election. Everything is viewed through that prism. The paper has a vision of how the country should be run. It may not be to everyone's tastes, but it is single-minded in pursuing that vision.

Finally, after two months of stasis followed by two months of 'crisis', it reluctantly concluded that the disloyal former chancellor who 'got us into this mess' was the man to get us out of it. It seemed not to recognise, let alone accept, that it had any part in creating the situation the country found itself in. Forever the optimist, it again proclaimed – on that 'new dawn' front page – that the 'Tory fightback starts here'.

This then, is the diary of the country's best-selling and most influential newspaper's tortuous journey from Johnson to Sunak via Truss. All the while believing that anyone but Boris was to blame for the upheaval in July and that everyone but the Mail was to blame for the chaos that ensued.

Daily Mail

FRIDAY, JULY 8, 2022 — Daily newspaper of the year — 80p

DAY TORIES LOST THEIR MARBLES

With a consoling hug from Carrie and Wilf, Boris is cast out by a party in the grip of collective hysteria. Keir Starmer is cock-a-hoop. Corks are popping in Brussels – and Moscow. And the Tories don't have a clue who should replace him

WHAT THE HELL HAVE THEY DONE?

By **Jason Groves** Political Editor

TORY MPs were last night warned they will 'rue the day' they forced Boris Johnson out.

After days of pressure from embittered foes and ambitious rivals, the Prime Minister yesterday announced he was standing down as party leader.

His departure fired the starting gun for a two-month race to be the next PM, with a string of political minnows suggesting they would

Turn to Page 4

SARAH VINE on the electrifying Boris/Gove psychodrama PAGES 8-9

Week 1

TRAITORS! ASSASSINS!

8 July

What the hell have they done?

Boris Johnson has resigned and the Mail is spitting with rage. Besides the splash, there are 18 inside pages, mostly focused on how great Johnson was and what a mistake it was to get rid of him. The first spread to look to the future is 12 and 13, which leads on foreign secretary Liz Truss cutting short her G20 trip to join the race to succeed him.

The leader drips with disdain for the nonentities and showboaters with their spasms of narcissistic self-righteousness who forced Johnson out, and asks 'Are we entering a time where only prime ministers who pay homage to the liberal, pro-Brussels metropolitan consensus can survive?'

Here was a man who had saved the country from a government of knuckle-dragging Corbynistas. Yet he had suffered a daily barrage of vitriolic and personal attacks from an unholy alliance of Leftist loudmouths, hand-wringing liberals and embittered Remainers, cheered on by the BBC, Sky, ITN, like-minded newspapers and deranged keyboard warriors on social media.

Yes, he broke the rules and dissembled, but his 'crimes' were hardly in the same league as Suez or taking the country to war on a pack of lies. Look at the achievements of this most charismatic and electable leader: breaking the Brexit impasse, overseeing the world-beating Covid vaccine, standing up for Ukraine.

Now, though, he has gone and the Mail surveys the field gathering to succeed him. It's full of traitors and plotters, but it seems to have spotted someone:

> *Nadhim Zahawi has a head for business, but treacherously knifed the Prime Minister hours after being appointed Chancellor.*

For standing up to Russia, Defence Secretary Ben Wallace is popular with the grassroots.

But could even his family pick him out of a line-up?

If ex-Health Secretary Sajid Javid and former Chancellor Rishi Sunak really were the paragons of integrity they claim, they'd have spent every waking hour respectively tackling record NHS waiting lists and the cost-of-living squeeze, not plotting to oust Mr Johnson.

By contrast, Liz Truss has performed with great aplomb at the Foreign Office, especially standing up to Brussels' bullying in her battle to fix the flawed Northern Ireland Protocol.

Page 20 Daily Mail, Friday, July 8, 2022

Boris faced his end with a rueful smile. But, by God, the Tory party could live to regret it

Daily Mail COMMENT

SO THE sun finally sets on Boris Johnson's premiership. Always a political outsider, he at last succumbed to the massed ranks of his enemies within the Westminster machine.

And how they crowed. The airwaves were thick with gloating nonentities denouncing Mr Johnson and signalling their own flawless virtue.

Yet after watching his valedictory speech outside Downing Street yesterday, the Tory MPs who shamefully conspired to topple the most charismatic and electable Conservative leader since Margaret Thatcher might already be asking themselves: What have we done?

These showboaters — many of whom owe their exalted positions to Mr Johnson — have contributed to a cacophony of largely manufactured outrage.

Now their spasms of narcissistic self-righteousness are abating, are they sure that turfing out the Prime Minister over what fundamentally amounts to trivialities is a well-judged course of action?

Yes, he broke rules and dissembled. And yes, the Chris Pincher sex pest affair and a string of other Westminster scandals — which played a part in multiple by-election drubbings — were deeply unedifying.

Propriety and integrity in politics — as in life — matter. Failure to adhere to such standards corrodes trust.

But let's be honest. Mr Johnson's 'crimes' were hardly in the same league as Suez — or indeed taking the country to war on a pack of lies.

However, once he had lost the confidence of most of his party — including several Cabinet ministers [illegible]

After they deserted him, he would have struggled to put together a government capable of delivering the ambitious agenda the country needs to face the myriad challenges ahead, from steering us through the cost of living crunch to the housing crisis and cracking down on crime.

And while it was admirable that he wanted to fight on for the sake of the country, he did the right thing by choosing to stand down with his dignity and reputation intact.

However, if the haters and cynics had expected to see a hangdog, remorseful Boris during his resignation address outside No 10, they were sorely disappointed.

Not for him the mournful demeanour of Theresa May, nor the tears of Margaret Thatcher as they announced their departure.

His words were gracious and carried not a hint of self-pity. Rather, he faced his political end with a rueful smile, accentuating the many positives of his time in Downing Street.

There were jokes about being trampled by the herd, but no bitterness or recrimination. Just thanks to the millions of voters who propelled him so dramatically into 'the best job in the world'.

And the hope that his One-Nation agenda would be pursued with equal vigour by his successor.

His bravura performance made it all the more baffling how on earth the Tory parliamentary party could have been so stupid as to defenestrate their greatest electoral asset.

It's truly astounding that they have dethroned someone who took them from a near-fatal nine per cent vote-share in a national election in 2019 to a stonking majority just months later.

So Mr Johnson's downfall poses another important question: Are we entering a time where only prime ministers who pay homage to the liberal, pro-Brussels, metropolitan consensus are able to survive?

For while he was loved and admired in the country for being different from the dreary career politicians around him, the political and broadcast media establishment hated him.

His arrival in No 10 broke their monopoly, smashed through their sullen Brexit impasse, snubbed the BBC, challenged the undemocratic arrogance of the civil service 'Blob' and humiliated his opponents.

Indeed, for Labour his triumphant march through the party's northern heartlands, saving the country from a government of knuckle-dragging Corbynistas, was a setback of existential proportions.

The response of Mr Johnson's enemies has been a daily barrage of vitriolic and personal attacks of a nature almost unprecedented in modern politics.

This unholy alliance of Leftist loudmouths, hand-wringing liberals and embittered Remainers have been cheered on by the BBC, Sky and ITN, which have abandoned all pretence of impartiality.

And their pathological anti-Boris mania has been amplified by like-minded newspapers and the deranged keyboard warriors on social media.

Worse still, this coup d'etat has been aided and abetted by Conservative MPs. Their logic, even those who bear grudges, is hard to fathom.

True, even Mr Johnson's most passionate supporters will sometimes have found his conduct hard to defend. But for all his travails, the Tories are still within touching distance of Labour in the polls.

So the flood of ministers suddenly determined to cast him into the outer darkness resembles less a rational decision than collective hysteria.

Have they forgotten the stunning achievements to the PM's name, short though his time in Downing Street might have been?

When Covid struck, the world-beating vaccine programme and furlough saved countless lives and jobs.

The levelling up agenda is revitalising parts of the country forgotten by successive governments.

And the doubters and cynics who say his presence in Downing Street has damaged Britain's reputation abroad are simply just wrong.

On Ukraine especially, he has displayed immense strength when other global leaders sought to appease Putin, and he has built solid bridges with other countries — both inside and outside the EU.

The only place he is really badmouthed is Brussels, still desperate for Brexit to fail and to see the British people punished for voting for it.

But another significant factor in his downfall was his apparent abandonment of Tory values.

His free-spending largesse alienated him from the Thatcherite wing of his party. Green levies and the rush to net zero contributed to the cost-of-living crunch. His tax rises led many backbenchers to question whether their boss was a Conservative at all.

But having guided the economy through the pandemic, he was immediately hit with an energy and inflation crisis.

He may not have got every call right, but any leader would have been faced with tough choices in such a crunch.

Labour are cock-a-hoop. They have a lacklustre leader and a policy vacuum.

The only way they can conceivably win the next election is by somehow persuading the country they would be less awful than the alternatives.

They wanted Mr Johnson toppled because they fear him at the ballot box — and rightly so.

Inevitably, there will come a period of chaos and confusion while a new leader is chosen.

But having committed regicide, are the Tories certain there is a better alternative to Boris?

Nadhim Zahawi has a head for business, but treacherously knifed the Prime Minister hours after being appointed Chancellor.

For standing up to Russia, Defence Secretary Ben Wallace is popular with the grassroots.

But could even his family pick him out of a line-up?

If ex-Health Secretary Sajid Javid and former Chancellor Rishi Sunak really were the paragons of integrity they claim, they'd have spent every waking hour respectively tackling record NHS waiting lists and the cost-of-living squeeze — not plotting to oust Mr Johnson.

By contrast, Liz Truss has performed with great aplomb at the Foreign Office, especially standing up to Brussels' bullying in her battle to fix the flawed Northern Ireland Protocol.

So while there are decent — if not formidable — candidates, none possesses Boris's vote-winning star quality.

But let's not be too pessimistic — yet. Leadership contests sometimes throw up previously disregarded though outstanding candidates.

The most important tasks for our next Prime Minister, whoever that is, dovetail: the ability to beat Labour and EU fanboy Sir Keir Starmer and the determination to defend Brexit to the hilt.

The glee of the Remainers at Boris's resignation, from sanctimonious hasbeen John Major to swivel-eyed Eurocrat Guy Verhofstadt, should be a warning alarm that in the wrong hands, the UK could be dragged back into the bloc.

The successful candidate should also run on an unashamedly True Blue ticket. Tax cuts. A proper energy policy that acknowledges the deficiencies of renewables and a pragmatic approach to fracking and nuclear.

Sort out the Northern Ireland Protocol. Stop the Channel migrants and the hold on Britain of foreign courts. Protect our statues and history. And stop agreeing to see this wonderful country through the prism of racism and inequality.

The outcome of this leadership race is crucial for the future of the Tory Party — and the country. After Mrs Thatcher was ousted in 1990, it led to hopeless John Major in No 10 – then the despair of 13 years of ruinous Labour rule.

By God, let's hope the Tories who connived to dethrone Mr Johnson don't similarly live to regret it.

9 July

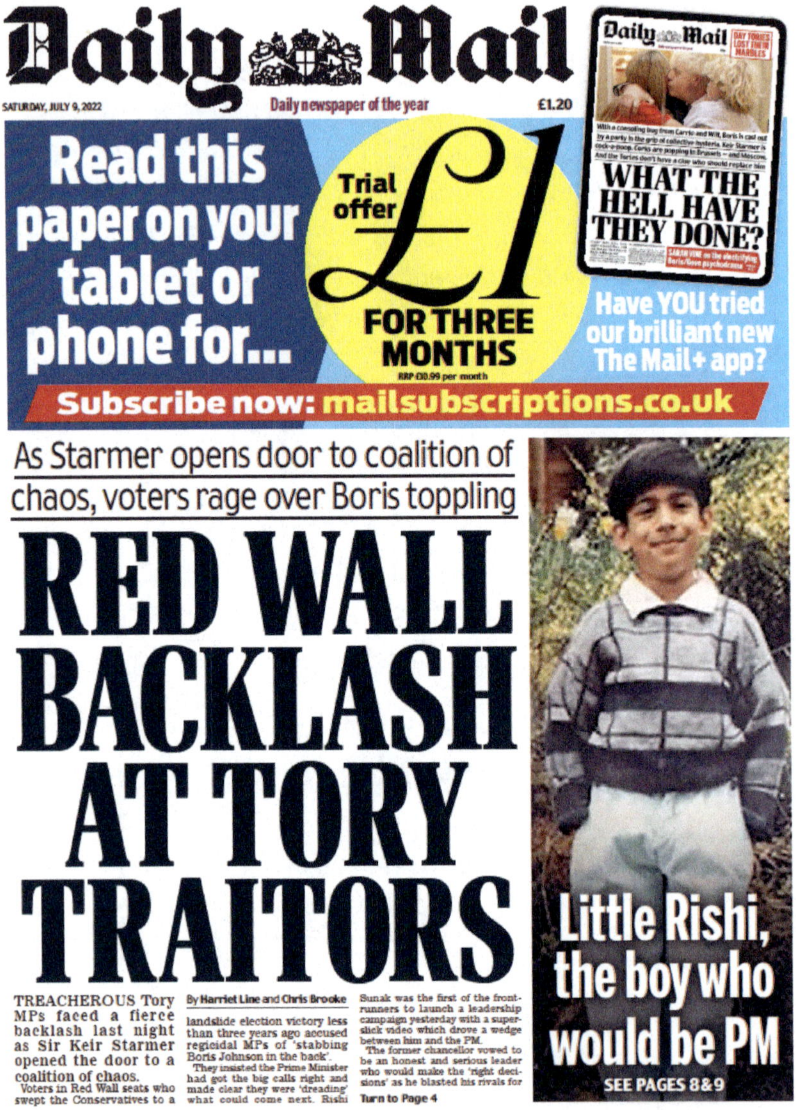

Daily Mail

SATURDAY, JULY 9, 2022 — Daily newspaper of the year — £1.20

Read this paper on your tablet or phone for... Trial offer £1 FOR THREE MONTHS RRP £10.99 per month

WHAT THE HELL HAVE THEY DONE?

Have YOU tried our brilliant new The Mail+ app?

Subscribe now: mailsubscriptions.co.uk

As Starmer opens door to coalition of chaos, voters rage over Boris toppling

RED WALL BACKLASH AT TORY TRAITORS

By Harriet Line and Chris Brooke

TREACHEROUS Tory MPs faced a fierce backlash last night as Sir Keir Starmer opened the door to a coalition of chaos.

Voters in Red Wall seats who swept the Conservatives to a landslide election victory less than three years ago accused regicidal MPs of 'stabbing Boris Johnson in the back'.

They insisted the Prime Minister had got the big calls right and made clear they were 'dreading' what could come next. Rishi Sunak was the first of the front-runners to launch a leadership campaign yesterday with a super-slick video which drove a wedge between him and the PM.

The former chancellor vowed to be an honest and serious leader who would make the 'right decisions' as he blasted his rivals for

Turn to Page 4

Little Rishi, the boy who would be PM

SEE PAGES 8&9

The knives are out for the Tory MPs who knifed Boris. No names are mentioned, but the third paragraph of the lead notes that Rishi Sunak was the first to declare himself a candidate and a picture of the former chancellor as a boy accompanies the story.

The five inside news pages consider potential candidates, with 'Slick Rishi' leading the main spread.

In the comment section, Mick Hume rails at the Brexit-loathing elite, while a Saturday essay by Andrew Neil quotes the Wall St Journal saying 'Britain is in the grip of an inflation crisis that Johnson made worse at every turn.' He also, by Neil's assessment, ran a No 10 operation that was 'dysfunctional, weak, unprofessional, aimless, populated by inexperienced political pygmies – all of which reflected the multiple flaws of its boss'.

Hang on. Wasn't he supposed to be the cruelly felled giant? The Comment column on the same page still thinks so. It seethes about the regicidal lunacy of self-obsessed Tory assassins who brutally despatched the man whose political stardust delivered the biggest Conservative majority since 1987.

They have 'gifted' Labour a huge opportunity and now there's a risk of a Labour-LibDem stitch-up that could keep the Conservatives out of power for decades.

To avoid this, the paper advises, Tories must not choose their next leader with 'undue haste' – because they'll get only one shot at this – and the clear message is 'don't rush to Rishi'.

> *After the candidates are whittled down to two, their policies and suitability for high office must be rigorously tested. After all, the Tories will only get one chance.*
>
> *Former chancellor Rishi Sunak yesterday became the first big beast to announce his candidacy. To his immense credit, he is an original Brexiteer, not an opportunist convert, and he emphasises Tory values - aspiration, hard work and family.*
>
> *However, some won't easily forgive his role in Mr Johnson's downfall.*

That reluctance to forgive will become entrenched in the coming weeks, with the 'some' turning to 'many' – and the Mail will be there at the side of these unforgivers, reminding them at every opportunity of the former chancellor's Brutus act. But never, of course, counting itself among their number.

Slick Rishi sprints out of starting gate

Sunak suggests rivals are telling 'fairy-tales' in sleek 3-minute launch promo

IN HIS OWN WORDS, A *VERY* GLOSSY PITCH TO BE PM

He wouldn't be much fun over dinner, but at least he'd split the bill fairly!

by Sarah Vine

For, as the leader continues, the paper is 'keeping an open mind' (in case Sunak wins and it has to campaign for him in the future). But it has a tick-list of 'true blue' policies: tax cuts, no backsliding on Brexit, tough on Northern Ireland, tighter borders to keep out the 'tsunami' of Channel migrants, and ending the wokery infecting our schools and public services.

11 July

Daily Mail

MONDAY, JULY 11, 2022

Daily newspaper of the year

80p

Read this paper on your tablet or phone

New offer 12 MONTHS FOR £65 (RRP £131.88)

AND GET FREE National Trust Family Day Pass (RRP £26) and 3,000 Nectar points worth £15

TERMS APPLY. See mailsubscriptions.co.uk for details.

Subscribe now: mailsubscriptions.co.uk/annual

Daily Mail

NEW NOW! 150 NECTAR POINTS EVERY MONTH FOR ALL MAIL+ SUBSCRIBERS

RED WALL BACKLASH AT TORY TRAITORS

As Truss launches her bid to be next PM, Sunak is forced to deny links to Boris's poison-spreading ex-adviser

RISHI CAUGHT IN CUMMINGS 'TOXIC SMEARS' STORM

The battle lines are being drawn, as the Mail leader puts it and the smearing of Sunak begins – in the sense that he is caught, according to the splash, in a 'Cummings toxic smears storm'. Sunak is not actually doing any smearing. It's Dirty Dom who is accused of saying nasty things about his potential rivals.

Liz Truss announces that she is standing, earning her the first spread with the heading 'I'll be the unity candidate', and a sidebar that starts 'forget Rishi'. The Mail is already gunning for Penny Mordaunt, who is accused of a gaffe and wokery on the second inside spread.

BATTLE FOR SOUL OF THE TORIES

Truss: I'll be the unity candidate

Foreign Secretary's vow to cut taxes and pull together Red and Blue Wall Tories as she pitches for leadership

YOUR AT-A-GLANCE GUIDE TO THE TOP TEN CONTENDERS

Forget Rishi's jam tomorrow, Liz wants help for voters now

By Jason Groves

The leader, which produces the first almost-endorsement for Truss, says that the choice the party makes will have seismic ramifications. If it picks the wrong person, Labour could seize power at the helm of a coalition of chaos and Britain would soon become an economic basket case.

Some want a 'coronation' of Sunak, but that's nonsense:

> *Six years ago, Theresa May had a coronation. Painfully for the Tories - and depressingly for the nation - that meant her disastrous weaknesses were not revealed until it was far too late.**

Now it's time to take another look at the latest candidates:

> *Mr Sunak insists tax cuts are not possible until we begin clearing our eye-watering Covid debts. Others, however, are determined to wrestle back the Tories' reputation as a low-tax party to spur growth.*
>
> *Pleasingly, several agree with the Mail's tireless campaign to spike the foolish and damaging national insurance hike, which callously hit voters at the moment the cost of living squeeze began biting viciously.*

Daily Mail

A party in flames and why it must be Theresa

Daily Mail COMMENT

TORY DAY OF TREACHERY

Most savage blood letting since fall of Thatcher as Gove knifes Boris in battle to be PM

Daily Mail GOOD HEALTH

CORONATION OF THERESA

After historic day she becomes PM tomorrow

Plans to heal rifts with Cabinet of all the talents

And she vows to make Brexit a huge success

Daily Mail JUNE 8TH

In a stunning move, Mrs May calls bluff of the 'game-playing' Remoaners (including 'unelected' Lords) with a snap election and vows to . . .

CRUSH THE SABOTEURS

Six years ago, the Mail ran another front page railing at Tory treachery. The victim that day was again Boris Johnson. A big blue puff at the top, pointing to another full-page leader, had a photograph of May and the headline 'A party in flames and why it must be Theresa'. At that point, there were still others in the race, but in the end there was no contest because her last rival standing, Andrea Leadsom, dropped out. The paper didn't seem too unhappy about 'the coronation of Theresa' and went on to project and protect her for three years, including urging her to 'crush the saboteurs' when she called an ill-advised general election in 2017.

Liz Truss is one. She's also hugely experienced and, as Foreign Secretary, has been strong on Ukraine and the Northern Ireland protocol. During her Westminster career, she has cleared every obstacle placed in front of her - much to her detractors' irritation...

Ex-health secretary Jeremy Hunt, however, is a non-runner for huge swathes of the party after calling for a brutal China-style lockdown and his pro-EU sympathies.

12 July

Daily Mail

TUESDAY, JULY 12, 2022 | Daily newspaper of the year | 80p

RISHI CAUGHT IN CUMMINGS 'TOXIC SMEARS' STORM

Read this paper on your tablet or phone

New offer 12 MONTHS FOR £65 (RRP £131.88)

AND GET FREE National Trust Family Day Pass (RRP £26) and 3,000 Nectar points worth £15

Subscribe now: mailsubscriptions.co.uk/annual

As rivals on the Tory Right battle each other – and Sunak still won't commit to instant tax cuts – Foreign Secretary's team issues warning

TRUSS: BACK ME OR IT'LL BE RISHI

The 'stop Rishi' campaign is in full flow as Truss makes the splash with 'Back me or it'll be Rishi' – the inference being that the Mail thinks that would be a bad thing. And to press home that point subtly, the previous day's 'Rishi smear' front page is republished next to the titlepiece as part of a puff for a subscription offer.

Truss is the main picture on the first spread of five inside pages, the second has Sunak promising to cut taxes after he's got a 'grip' on inflation (the Mail's quote marks) but being given the cold shoulder by Lord Frost*, who WON'T back him for No 10.

BATTLE FOR SOUL OF THE TORIES

Rivals scramble to get on ballot

I'm not a contender, says Mogg

Priti told not to run and split the Right

Penny beats Rishi in poll of Tory members

Kemi: Free speech is cornerstone of UK

Suella: Choose me for my love of Britain, not my skin colour

BATTLE FOR SOUL OF THE TORIES

New pledge after leadership rivals throw down the gauntlet

Sunak: I WILL cut tax ... but only when I've got 'grip' on inflation

It's a cold shoulder from Frost

Former chief Brexit negotiator WON'T back Rishi for No10

ALEX BRUMMER

Saj sweats as he dodges questions about using tax havens

Now Zahawi faces £30m loan claims

HENRY DEEDES SKETCH

A gasp and a thump. The Chancellor had a fainter on his hands

**David Frost was Boris Johnson's chief Brexit negotiator, delivering a deal he later repudiated. Never having been elected, he was ennobled by Johnson so that he could be brought into government. He resigned – from the Cabinet, not the Lords – at the end of 2021 over Covid strategy and concerns about the government's 'direction of travel'.*

Since then, he has assumed the mantle of a modern-day Oracle of Delphi. With a weekly column in the Daily Telegraph from which to dispense his wisdom on Tory policy and politicians, his every pronouncement is treated with deference by the rightwing media.

A small downpage story about polls suggesting that Mordaunt would beat Sunak in the final runoff may look insignificant, but...watch this space.

The leader – 'Tory activists must be given a proper choice' – notes that only Sunak is making a virtue of not cutting tax until inflation is under control and is sceptical of some other candidates' promises. Sunak is the strong favourite, so far, but the Mail says his record on taxation is shameful and that he has 'blotted his copybook' with his 'key role' in toppling Johnson.

> *If the Right of the Tory party want to stop a Sunak coronation, they must unite behind a single candidate to avoid the risk of splitting their vote. It is imperative that aspirants look long and hard at themselves – and each other – and ask honestly: Who is best placed to beat him?*

13 July

Daily Mail

WEDNESDAY, JULY 13, 2022 — Daily newspaper of the year — 80p

As Tory Right rallies to Liz Truss, Rees-Mogg launches a scathing attack in Mail on Sunak's economic record

RISHI BLASTED ON 'SOCIALIST' TAXES

By **Claire Ellicott**
Political Correspondent

THE Tory Right rallied behind Liz Truss last night with a series of brutal attacks on Rishi Sunak.

Jacob Rees-Mogg accused the former chancellor of raising tax to 'socialist' levels and 'squandering' their party's record on the economy.

His Cabinet colleague Nadine Dorries accused Mr Sunak's team of 'dirty tricks' and trying to rig the leadership race.

Eight candidates yesterday attracted the 20 nominations they needed to stay in the race to succeed Boris Johnson as prime minister. Tory MPs will today vote on who advances from Mr Sunak, Miss Truss, Penny Mordaunt, Tom Tugendhat, Kemi Badenoch, Nadhim Zahawi, Jeremy Hunt and Suella Braverman.

Former health secretary Sajid Javid, who knifed Mr Johnson last week, was humiliated yesterday after failing to secure enough backers and had to pull out.

In an article for today's Daily Mail, Mr Rees-Mogg writes: 'Sunak has squandered the Conservative Party's decade-long effort to build a competitive tax regime and it will be the French and the Americans who will benefit, instead of the British people.

'With Liz Truss as prime minister, we will

Turn to Page 4

Has Priti just been told how many backers PM's assassin Javid got?

SEE PAGES 10-11

Nominations close and, to the Mail's delight, 'Boris assassin' Sajid Javid fails to secure the necessary 20 backers, leaving eight in the ring.

Page 4 BATTLE FOR SOUL OF THE TORIES Daily Mail, Wednesday, July 13, 2022

She fought Rishi's tax hikes and the Whitehall blob – that's why I'm backing Liz Truss

by Jacob Rees-Mogg

FOR the next Prime Minister we need a candidate who is committed to realising the benefits of Brexit, with a strong economic agenda designed to bring down inflation and restore growth, as well as the determination to cut Whitehall down to size.

In my role as Brexit Opportunities Minister nobody has given me more support than Liz Truss. Without her backing we would have imposed border controls in July that would have increased the cost of food.

She also wants to see a sunset on retained EU law, unlike the Treasury, which has argued to keep tax policy in lockstep with the European Union in perpetuity.

Liz showed her mettle as International Trade Secretary. She spearheaded the trade agenda, setting in motion brand new trade deals with Australia and New Zealand, as well as expanding and improving on countless EU deals with countries like Mexico and Japan. We may have a trade deal with India this year, thanks to the foundations laid by her.

As Foreign Secretary, she has been one of the strongest and most convincing advocates for Brexit in Government. Apart from her support for me, she faced off against the erstwhile Chancellor Rishi Sunak who tried to stop her and the Prime Minister securing the integrity of the United Kingdom by tackling the Northern Ireland Protocol.

With global supply chains under strain, there is no candidate I trust more than Liz to actually deliver the economic reforms which will cut prices, increase growth and resilience, and tackle inflation once and for all.

Her political philosophy is one with which all Conservatives should agree: putting the voter, the taxpayer and the consumer first, reforming the economy to help British businesses to compete with the whole world, and trusting businesses, entrepreneurs and the free market to grow the economy free of interference from overbearing regulators.

She knows how to get the most out of Whitehall and tackle the blob: in 2020 she banned the Civil Service from using pernicious unconscious bias training and improved the way in which the Government addresses inequality, by including economic and geographical factors, instead of the crude methods preferred by woke officials and the Labour Party.

Britain faces grave challenges today. Liz has rejected the path that Rishi Sunak wanted to take us down.

She opposed his breaking of our manifesto promise, with the National Insurance hike when the British people had barely recovered from the shock of the pandemic. She opposed him raising the tax burden to the highest since the socialism of 1950s Labour. While the economy was at its most fragile, she opposed his plan to raise Corporation Tax by around 30 per cent next year, which will deter investment and economic growth when we need it most.

Sunak has squandered the Conservative Party's decade-long efforts to build a competitive tax regime and it will be the French and the Americans who will benefit, instead of the British people. With Liz Truss as Prime Minister, we will have the best chance to undo these errors and right Britain's course.

LIZ has the most compelling and credible vision for how to restore our economy to growth, tackle inflation and pay for public services without taxing the public into submission.

Outside the European Union, we can harness the benefits of Brexit, remove redundant EU regulations from our books and make businesses more efficient and dynamic – and the British people more prosperous. This is the agenda which will restore the British economy to health and rebuild the public's trust in the Conservatives.

It is undoubtedly true that the Conservative Party has suffered a difficult period after an extraordinary victory by Boris Johnson in 2019. Boris gave our party a mandate to deliver on the promises of Brexit and unleash the economic potential of the entire United Kingdom.

For the good of the country, Conservative Party members and all MPs, we must choose the candidate who will complete this task, and respect the choice of our voters who made their decision in December 2019. I believe that the best way of fulfilling this mandate is by voting for Liz Truss as leader of the Conservative Party.

With Sunak looking the front-runner before the first ballot, Jacob Rees-Mogg throws his weight behind Truss and writes a page 4 piece, attacking the former chancellor's tax record. This also makes the splash as 'Sunak blasted on "socialist" taxes'.

The first of three inside news spreads is devoted to Javid schadenfreude, the second has Sunak defending his record alongside a colour piece headed 'Folksy sincerity oozed out of golden boy's every pore'. The third is an attack on 'Part-time Penny', who apparently doesn't know what a woman is.

BATTLE FOR SOUL OF THE TORIES

'Part-time Penny' jibe as Mordaunt is hit by new woke accusations

Jo Cox cut from campaign video

No 10 thwarts Labour bid to oust Boris now

COMMENTARY By Louise Perry

A tale of two female Tory candidates – only one of whom can tell you what a woman is

BATTLE FOR SOUL OF THE TORIES

Betrayed the PM? No, I served him loyally, Rishi tells critics

HENRY DEEDES SKETCH

Folksy sincerity oozed out of golden boy's every pore

Badenoch's swipe at rivals' tax cut claims

Hopefuls dodge reporters' questions

A short leader says that the Right must coalesce* around one candidate with one thing in mind: who is best placed to beat Keir Starmer.

*'Coalesce' is a must-have word on any Mail leader bingo card. There is a one in ten chance of it appearing in any editorial or OpEd column related to the Tory leadership.

14 July

Daily Mail

THURSDAY, JULY 14, 2022 | Daily newspaper of the year | 80p

RISHI BLASTED ON 'SOCIALIST' TAXES

As Rishi tops first leadership poll and Mordaunt surges into second, Foreign Secretary issues an urgent warning...

UNITE NOW OR WE LOSE, TRUSS TELLS TORY RIGHT

By Jason Groves
Political Editor

THE Tory Right was under pressure to unite behind Liz Truss last night amid warnings Penny Mordaunt could exploit their divisions.

The Foreign Secretary emerged as the leading candidate of the Conservative Right yesterday after securing 50 votes in the first round of the contest to succeed Boris Johnson.

But she trailed Establishment favourite Rishi Sunak, who won 88 votes, and Miss Mordaunt, who stunned rivals by picking up 67.

A shock poll of Tory members yesterday suggested Miss Mordaunt holds a substantial lead among the grassroots who will ultimately decide the contest. Bookmakers last night installed her as favourite to become prime minister.

Her new status is likely to bring intense scrutiny and last night she was facing questions on whether she had changed her 'woke' views on trans rights in order to win support.

An ally of Miss Truss accused Miss

Turn to Page 4

Crest of a wave: Penny Mordaunt yesterday

New favourite Penny under fire for 'lies' on trans views

SEE PAGES 8-9

The first MPs' ballot eliminates Jeremy Hunt and Nadhim Zahawi. Sunak tops the poll with 88 votes and Mordaunt is second with 67. For the Mail, the most important thing is that Liz Truss garnered 50 votes. And it's what she – rather than the two ahead of her – has to say that makes the splash.

The story says that bookmakers have installed Mordaunt as favourite and that her 'new status' was likely to bring intense scrutiny. Questions were already being raised about whether she had changed her woke views to win support. The main picture is not of Truss telling the Right to unite, but of Mordaunt under fire for 'lies' on trans views.

BATTLE FOR SOUL OF THE TORIES

Backlash at Penny's shift in trans storm

Truss ally claims Mordaunt is 'telling lies' over changing views

'Reversing her stance to win over members'

'Might have ruined her chances'

If she won't stand up for the rights of women, she'll never get my vote

by Sarah Vine

PM4PM

Bookies' favourite only 1-in-9 could pick out in a crowd

ANALYSIS By Jason Groves

There's a lot more of that in the body of the leadership coverage, but Mordaunt also shows up on page 4 – without fanfare – in a bylined piece, 'Why I will ALWAYS fight for this great nation', talking about the importance of maintaining and increasing defence spending, the battle for Ukraine, and why she wants the top job. Then it's back to business as usual with more Mordaunt backlash on page 8.

Truss promising to hit the ground [running] brings up the rear of the coverage, but not before a double-page 'exposé' by Andrew Pierce, headlined 'Is a shadowy ex-sex party organiser...secretly helping Team Rishi?' If that's not enticing enough, the strapline is bound to lure you in: 'Sunak has already had to deny his campaign is in cahoots with Cummings, but it gets even murkier'.

Sunak tops first poll, but is he losing momentum?

'Almost no chance of winning'

... as Zahawi and Hunt crash out of running

'There was a fifth column inside No 10'

'All paths lead back to Cummings'

Sunak's already had to deny his campaign's in cahoots with Cummings. But it gets even murkier

Is a shadowy ex-sex party organiser – who warned Boris 'Quit or we'll get you out' – now secretly helping Team Rishi?

ANDREW PIERCE EXPOSÉ

'Rishi clearly didn't want to help Boris'

Sunak ally hits out over Downing Street parties

Machiavellian manoeuvres behind plot to topple Boris... and how they all lead to Rishi

Andrew Pierce reporting

This is quite the guilt-by-association hatchet job. And it has absolutely nothing to do with the swingers' parties of the headline and intro. They happened 20 years ago. This is about a spider's web of friendships and alliances including Dominic Cummings, former No 10 policy chief Munira Mirza and her husband Dougie Smith (the ex-sex party organiser), Sunak's chief of staff Liam Booth-Smith, and Oliver Dowden.

They were all, according to Pierce, part of an attempted coup designed to move Sunak next door in Downing Street. This started, Pierce writes, back in February when Mirza, who had worked for Johnson since his time as Mayor of London, resigned over the prime minister's PMQs jibe that Keir Starmer had spent most of his time as DPP 'not prosecuting Jimmy Savile'. Indeed, Pierce wrote as much at the time: 'Machiavellian manoeuvres behind plot to topple

Boris – and how they all lead to Rishi'. Now he's reheating the same feast, with a few extra tasty side dishes.

So if Mordaunt and Sunak are beyond the pale, who should the Tories turn to? The Mail's first leader, calling for the Tory Right to 'get real', has a suggestion:

> *Truss has distinguished herself in Cabinet and on the international stage. She is the obvious choice for those who don't want Sunak or Mordaunt.*

The second editorial, 'Questions for Penny' urges Mordaunt to 'come clean' on her views on gender recognition; the third, headlined 'Defying the doomsters', notes that the British economy 'seems to be doing rather well'.

Week 2

BAD PENNY KEEPS TURNING UP

Daily Mail

FRIDAY, JULY 15, 2022 Daily newspaper of the year 80p

Subscribe now: mailsubscriptions.co.uk/annual

Read this paper on your tablet or phone

New offer 12 MONTHS FOR £65 (RRP £131.88)

AND GET FREE National Trust Family Day Pass (RRP £26) and 3,000 Nectar points worth £15

UNITE NOW OR WE LOSE, TRUSS TELLS TORY RIGHT

AS SHE'S SURPRISE FAVOURITE TO BE PM

MORDAUNT UNDER THE MICROSCOPE

- Her old boss Lord Frost says he has 'grave reservations' about her as PM
- Rival Braverman backs Truss and says Penny doesn't stand up for women in trans debate
- Questions over her backers and lack of Cabinet support

By Claire Ellicott and Kumail Jaffer

PENNY Mordaunt came under fire last night as senior Tories questioned whether she has what it takes to be Prime Minister.

The trade minister cemented her position as a front-runner in the party's leadership race after a second round of MPs' votes yesterday.

But on a day of extraordinary blue-on-blue attacks, Miss Mordaunt was under

Turn to Page 4

Penny for her thoughts: Tory leadership front-runner Miss Mordaunt

15 July

Suella Braverman is eliminated in the next MPs' ballot. Sunak is still ahead, Mordaunt still second, Truss still third, but gaining.

Yesterday's splash that Mordaunt was likely to face intense scrutiny turns out to have shown astonishing foresight, for here she is again on the front page under the headline 'Mordaunt under the microscope'. She has cemented her place as front-runner, but 'senior Tories'* are questioning whether she's got what it takes to be prime minister. And her former boss Lord Frost has grave doubts about her suitability. So that's it then.

Inside, two of the three news spreads are devoted to attacking her. The first is her 'failure' to fight for women, the second another Andrew Pierce exposé. After yesterday's Sunak masterpiece, this one is headlined 'Her career has come under little scrutiny to date. So Tory MPs should read this troubling dossier before putting a cross against her name again'.

After all this vitriol, who'll put Humpty Dumpty Tory party back together again?

ANALYSIS By Jason Groves

Mordaunt in free Press row

MORDAUNT UNDER THE MICROSCOPE

Her career to date has come under little scutiny. So Tory MPs should read this troubling dossier before putting a cross next to her name again

ANDREW PIERCE EXPOSÉ

Much of her book is a paean to wokery

Ministers question her work ethic

Pierce tells us that Mordaunt is named after a warship, has a twin brother and eight cats, and that she took part in the reality TV series Splash. She also co-authored a book that Pierce describes as a paean to wokery in which she says the MBE and OBE should be abolished, the House of Lords should be elected** and that she doesn't like It Ain't Half Hot Mum. That she flew to the Hay on Wye festival to promote the book in a helicopter 'says a great deal about her vaunting ambition'. But her greatest sin is to have shown inconsistency on trans issues – for which she has been subjected to more than a little scrutiny from the Mail in recent days. It has also already reported the book, the dislike of It Ain't Half Hot Mum, the helicopter flight and the reality show.

**The definition of a 'senior Tory' is fluid. It could be someone in a position of authority, but not necessarily. It could be someone who used to be a minister (no matter how briefly) or someone who has been in Parliament for a long time without progressing from the back benches. Sometimes 'senior Tories' are named – in this case they are chief secretary to the Treasury Simon Clarke and Iain Duncan Smith – but more often they are anonymous. IDS is a regular, as are John Redwood and, of course, Lord Frost. They are almost always Brexiteers and if you were one of John Major's 'bastards' you probably qualify. Major himself doesn't, despite having been a Conservative prime minister for seven years. He should shut up and go away.*

The concerns of 'senior Tories' are to be taken seriously. Unless they are disloyal. Like Michael Gove, a Brexiteer and probably the most senior Tory of the current cohort never to be so described.

***The Mail, incidentally, has frequently criticised the honours system, especially for cronyism – although it seems to have no problems with Lords Frost and Cruddas – and previously described the Lords as a 'House of unelected wreckers'. But that was before Paul Dacre was lining up for a peerage.*

BATTLE FOR SOUL OF THE TORIES

Frost & Suella booster for Liz

She wins vital new backing from party's Right as Kemi told to give way

HENRY DEEDES SKETCH

LIZ FOR LEADER

She gave a true blue message, but her joints could do with a squirt of oil

So, when did Rishi decide to knife old boss Boris?

I feel like a prom queen, says Tom as he's wooed by all sides

The third spread has a 'booster' for Liz and her 'true blue' message as the Oracle Frost gives her the nod and Braverman is poised to back her too. There's also another gentle reminder of Sunak's treachery with 'So, when did Rishi decide to knife old boss Boris?'

The leader sustains the assault on Mordaunt and encourages Kemi Badenoch to step aside to clear the way for Truss, who 'significantly' has the backing of the Oracle:

> *A candidate who does have a strong and demonstrable Cabinet record is Foreign Secretary Liz Truss.*
>
> *She embodies the values of traditional Conservatism - low tax, aspirational, meritocratic, anti-woke. And unlike the other front-runners, she remained loyal to Boris to the end. Significantly, she has the endorsement of Lord Frost.*

16 July

FREE SUN LOTION

*Online access, Mail account and one Unique Number required. £3.95 P&P payable. Terms apply. SEE PAGE 48

Daily Mail

SATURDAY, JULY 16, 2022

Daily newspaper of the year

£1.20

EXCLUSIVE INTERVIEW

Camilla on milestone birthdays, Charles the grandad – and 'flipping mobiles' at dinner table

SEE PAGES 8-10

Pledge to help those who take time off work to care for loved ones

LIZ TAX BOOST FOR FAMILIES

By John Stevens Deputy Political Editor

FAMILIES would be offered a tax break of up to £2,500 under plans being considered by Liz Truss.

The Tory leadership contender today pledges a radical overhaul of the tax system if she becomes prime minister.

She wants to ensure parents are not penalised for taking time out of work to look after family members. Couples with young children or caring responsibilities would be among those able to share their personal tax allowances under the plan.

The Foreign Secretary yesterday promised a tax-cutting bonanza worth more than £30billion in a dramatic bid to get her campaign to succeed Boris Johnson back on track.

She vowed to axe green levies on energy bills, cancel a planned corporation tax rise and reverse a hike in national insurance.

And Miss Truss says she would take immediate action to start 'putting money back into people's pockets' as they struggle with surging inflation.

Speaking to the Daily Mail, she vows to go further by launching an immediate review of the tax

Turn to Page 4

MORDAUNT UNDER THE MICROSCOPE

I like Penny, but her as PM fills me with horror, says old boss Amanda Platell

SEE PAGE 21

Feeling the heat? Penny Mordaunt yesterday

Liz Truss is back on the front after giving the Mail an interview in which she says she is considering changes to the tax system so that parents can take time off work to care for their families. Again, this story is accompanied by a photograph of Penny Mordaunt, again 'under the microscope' – this time with Amanda Platell saying that the thought of her being PM fills her with horror.

BATTLE FOR SOUL OF THE TORIES

TRUSS LAYS INTO RISHI ON TAX RISES

In first of three TV debates, they clash over cost of living as Sunak's Tory rivals vow to spike the hike

'Billion-pound promises'

SARAH VINE
View from the sofa

'Talking about the Army too much'

No clear winner... but Penny didn't make the splash she'd hoped for

Do you trust MPs? No, says audience

The three inside spreads have Truss 'laying into Rishi' in the first TV debate, Mordaunt being incapable of organising a tea party and a Sunak 'petrol bombshell' – he apparently wanted a green levy on fuel that was blocked by No 10. A sidebar on this spread says that as a student he was regarded as not ruthless enough for politics '– then he knifed Boris'. Another black mark is that he has been endorsed by China.

BATTLE FOR SOUL OF THE TORIES

Rishi's petrol bombshell: He wanted green tax on fuel (but No 10 blocked it)

'Explored many options'

... and he put a stop on licence fee review, leaked letter shows

'Implement a new way of funding'

Oxford pals thought he wasn't ruthless enough for politics... then he knifed Boris!

The endorsement that nobody wanted: Beijing backs Sunak

'Clear and pragmatic view'

The leader repeats the mantra that we shouldn't be having this contest, Boris was and is best, his political assassination shaming the tawdry plotters who wielded the knives; Mordaunt is hopeless; Badenoch too inexperienced. Sunak was an excellent chancellor through Covid, but brought us the highest taxes for 70 years.

The other candidate of proven ability in a range of Cabinet posts is Liz Truss.

As she showed in last night's debate, she's not as polished a public performer as some others. However, call us old-fashioned but at this paper we value substance over style.

In that department, she has consistently shown her mettle. She has negotiated trade deals around the world, stood up to the EU over Northern Ireland and has been unfailingly resolute on Ukraine.

Today she unveils imaginative plans to ease the financial burden on hard-pressed families and carers with targeted tax cuts. Along with pledges to reverse the National Insurance rise, hold down corporation tax and scrap some green levies, she offers true Tory solutions to real-world problems.

Not only is she the candidate with the most impressive CV, but also the one who most embodies the Conservative principles of aspiration, family values and low taxes.

18 July

Daily Mail

MONDAY, JULY 18, 2022

Daily newspaper of the year

80p

LIZ TAX BOOST FOR FAMILIES

Read this paper on your tablet or phone

New offer 12 MONTHS FOR £65 (RRP £131.88)

AND GET FREE National Trust Family Day Pass (RRP £26) and 3,000 Nectar points worth £15

Subscribe now: mailsubscriptions.co.uk/annual

MORDAUNT FLOUTED No10 BAN TO MEET BOYCOTTED GROUP

She's condemned for 'dodgy judgment' ahead of MPs' vote today – after Tory rivals clash in feisty TV debate

The 'stop Penny' juggernaut ploughs on with a lead on her meeting the leader of the Muslim Council of Britain when the Government had a policy of 'not engaging' with the group. The meeting had taken place 17 months earlier and she tweeted about it at the time, but it is now splashworthy.

Inside coverage includes two spreads; one expands on the criticism of Mordaunt, the other considers the previous night's TV debate, with 'Liz lashing out at Rishi'.

MORDAUNT UNDER THE MICROSCOPE

Even Labour had blacklisted them

Muslim Council of Britain was linked to Hamas – and threats against our Armed Forces – in 2009... so why did a Navy reservist hold talks with its new leader?

The reasons behind the official boycott

This should sink HMS Mordaunt
Dominic Lawson – Page 16

Penny on trans U-turn row: I'm a victim of smears

How she showed support for Extinction Rebellion protests

DOES LEAK SHOW PENNY DID BACK GENDER SELF-ID?

BATTLE FOR SOUL OF THE TORIES

Liz lashes out at slick Rishi after his swipe in new video

RISHI & BREXIT
A short history

Their acid exchanges

Tory poll: Truss beats main rivals in run-off

Again, no clear winner, but Liz made ground... and Penny just seemed cross with everyone

SARAH VINE
View from the sofa

These are followed by a single page, headlined 'Tax cuts aren't a fairytale Rishi'. This is illustrated with caricature of Sunak that is attributed to Tory donor Lord Cruddas, who is said to have circulated it in social media posts describing the former chancellor as a rat, a little weasel, a treacherous snake, a backstabber and Fishy Rishi.

These insults are repeated with neither condemnation nor endorsement. That is, shall we say, quite unusual for the Mail, which would get very cross when Joe Lycett mocked Truss on Laura Kuenssberg's TV show in September and when the Economist likened her to a lettuce in October.

As economic experts say inflation will give Treasury a £60billion boost by 2025, it's proof positive that...

Tax cuts aren't a fairytale, Rishi!

By Lucy White

THE HAND THAT WIELDS THE KNIFE

SHALL NEVER WEAR THE CROWN

Tory donor to cut funding if Sunak wins

By John Stevens
Deputy Political Editor

'NI hike was a mistake'

Cop26 minister may quit

Kemi: We will stop policing Twitter spats and focus on what matters

By Deputy Political Editor

'Public expect police to deal with criminals'

Tugendhat: I'm in race to win it

Further back, the main item in Andrew Pierce's diary column is 'That's rich! Do Sunak's expenses expose his plot?' It seems the former chancellor's claims for staffing costs had dropped from £152,000 in 2020-21 to £2,988 last year. Only Jacob Rees-Mogg had charged less. 'An act of selfless generosity by Sunak?' asks Pierce, 'Or does his decision more than 12 months ago to start paying for his staff himself indicate he was on manoeuvres as far back as then?'

The leader again mourns the departure of Johnson; the charismatic and vote-winning PM would have 'wiped the floor with Keir Starmer (aka Captain Crasheroony Snoozefest*)' and the fringe parties hoping to join him in a 'broad Left coalition of Bedlam'.

Alas, the Tories had chosen strife and self-mutilation over stability. Whoever they pick now will be second best, but MPs mustn't make a bad situation worse by denying the grassroots a 'real' choice. Sunak and Mordaunt are too like-minded and Mordaunt is unsuitable. Badenoch or Truss must get on the final ballot paper, preferably Truss.

> *Mr Sunak repeated his warning that to cut taxes now would be unwise, promising only jam tomorrow. Does he understand that people are facing genuine hardship?*
>
> *In contrast, Miss Truss demonstrated her passionate commitment to low-tax, small state Conservatism, by promising to ease the burden on hard-pressed families immediately, rather than waiting for some hypothetical future date.*

**The Mail makes no attempt to conceal its hatred of the Labour party and the broader 'Left', seeing them as socialist cranks who would ruin the country with their 'coalition of chaos'. But it has special reserves of contempt for Keir Starmer and keeps a compendium of insults for him, including that he is 'an ocean-going dud' and 'Mogadon man'.*

The current favourite – from a paper that demands that MPs stop behaving like children – comes straight out of the school playground: Captain Crasheroony (today with a 'y', but subsequently with 'ie') Snoozefest. The sobriquet was coined by Boris Johnson at PMQs the previous Wednesday and appeared in the Mail 13 times over the following four months. Indeed, the paper picked up and ran not just with the nickname, but the whole Johnson quote – that any one of the candidates to succeed him as PM would 'wipe the floor with Captain Crasheroony Snoozefest'.

This captain replaced Starmer's earlier incarnation as 'Captain Hindsight', another Johnson invention adopted enthusiastically by the Mail. Johnson stopped using it, though, after he apologised to MPs in January for attending a party at Downing Street. He said he had thought it was a work event, 'but, with hindsight, I should have sent everyone back inside'.

19 July

Daily Mail

TUESDAY, JULY 19, 2022 Daily newspaper of the year 80p

Sunny day snowflake Britain had a meltdown

Schools close, workers stay home and shops shut ++ Trains, Tubes and flights cancelled ++ And 'extreme heat' will be worse today

SEE PAGES 6-7

But it's not too hot for a bearskin...

...and Charles didn't even take his jacket and tie off!

MORDAUNT'S No10 BID HITS BUFFERS

By **Claire Ellicott**
Political Correspondent

Her vote goes down in latest leadership poll as Sunak's lead soars – and Tory Right STILL split

PENNY Mordaunt's bid to become Tory leader dramatically stalled last night after she lost support among fellow MPs.

In a close-fought third round of voting, Rishi Sunak extended his lead to become clear favourite in the race to replace Boris Johnson.

Miss Mordaunt remained in second place on 82 votes, but lost one of her backers. Foreign Secretary Liz Truss, in third, closed the gap after gaining seven supporters to secure 71 votes.

Little-known ex-equalities minister Kemi Badenoch was fourth on 58, up nine on the previous round of voting last Thursday. Just 24 votes separate the three women, any of whom could win the battle to be one of the two short-listed candidates who are put forward

Turn to Page 4

Tom Tugenhat is eliminated in the fourth ballot. Sunak, Mordaunt and Truss are still the top three, but Mordaunt's vote has declined, giving the Mail its splash angle.

There is surprise, however, that Sunak remains so far in front, since supporters of Suella Braverman, who was eliminated in the previous round, were expected to line up behind Truss and that didn't seem to have happened. There are therefore suggestions inside that the Sunak camp might be using dirty tricks to ensure that he doesn't face Truss in the final vote. This has shades of the final MPs' ballot in 2019 when Boris Johnson supporters were said to have 'lent' their votes to Jeremy Hunt to make sure Michael Gove didn't make the final cut. The Mail doesn't mention this though.

BATTLE FOR SOUL OF THE TORIES

Could Rishi exploit lead to pick his own preferred opponent?

Jason Groves

Final debate axed as Sunak and Truss pull out after bitter rows

LITTLEJOHN

by Richard Kay

Rise and rise of the anti-woke crusader who could become Labour's WORST nightmare

'It was an amazing privilege to be a British citizen'

'My passport was like Willy Wonka's golden ticket'

Truss herself is strangely absent from the day's goodies. The first spread is dominated by the rise of Badenoch, and the second is devoted to a further attack on Mordaunt – 'Another boss blasts Part-time Penny'.

MORDAUNT UNDER THE MICROSCOPE

Another boss blasts 'Part-time Penny'

Tory hopeful is accused of shirking duties to focus on bid for leadership

She defended the Iraq 'witch-hunt' against UK troops

Mordaunt dismissed warning over removing the word 'mother'

Rejected by the Red Wall

Boris is too woke, complained outspoken activist on her team

And there's more blasting on the third – this time by barnstorming Johnson, taking aim at the plotters who unseated him. He gave this 'bravura' address in the Commons, but is photographed rocking a Top Gun Tom Cruise look sitting in, and walking away from, a warplane.

WHAT THE HELL HAVE THEY DONE?

Bravura Boris's blast at plotters

In what could be his final Commons appearance as PM, he takes aim at 'The Revengers' - and shows Tory MPs what they'll miss

The latest parade of pretenders

I had 3 happy years in the cockpit

Savour his farewell bon mots

As he spoke, the Labour benches steamed like rows of cooked clams

HENRY DEEDES

SKETCH

That word is back in the leader as the Mail tells the Right to back Truss:

> *Traditionalist MPs must wise up and coalesce behind one candidate. Miss Truss is the obvious choice, given her strong track record and she is best placed to overtake Miss Mordaunt.*

20 July

Daily Mail

WEDNESDAY, JULY 20, 2022 | Daily newspaper of the year | 80p

HOTTEST UK DAY EVER 40.3°

Nightmare of the wildfires

London's burning: Terrified residents fled as these homes went up in flames yesterday in Wennington to the east of the capital. Major fires also hit Upminster, Wembley, Croydon and Dartford as the UK sweltered in temperatures over 40C, the hottest ever recorded here. SEE PAGES 6-11

As surge makes Liz bookies' favourite to be PM, supporters tell rival camps don't 'lend' votes to fix today's final ballot

TRUSS ALLIES WARN: NO DIRTY BACKROOM DEALS

By Jason Groves and Harriet Line

ALLIES of Liz Truss last night warned Rishi Sunak against engaging in 'dirty backroom deals'.

The Foreign Secretary enjoyed a surge in support in yesterday's penultimate leadership ballot of Conservative MPs.

But her backers fear the former chancellor's team may try to 'fix' the final vote today to ensure he does not face a candidate from the Tory Right in the run-off decided by party members.

They say she has the momentum to make the last two against Mr Sunak after picking up 15 votes yesterday and closing the gap to Penny Mordaunt to just six. And they pointed to a YouGov survey showing that – head to head – she would beat Mr Sunak by a comfortable margin of 54:35.

A former minister also suggested that Mr Sunak, who he is backing, would

Turn to Page 4

Badenoch is eliminated, leaving just Sunak, Mordaunt and Truss in the race. For some time, polls have suggested that either of the women would beat Sunak in the final vote and the Mail is determined that it should be Liz.

BATTLE FOR SOUL OF THE TORIES

Truss is now the Tory grassroots favourite

Mordaunt loses top spot and Rishi trails behind in new poll

OUT

IN

BBC will host live debate on Monday

'He loses by wide margins'

Vote? Let's have a show of fans

ANALYSIS By JASON GROVES

Liz should now make the final two. But Sunak's team is full of Masters of the Dark Arts – and no one would ever know...

Hopefuls 'must tackle cost of living crunch to halt financial cataclysm'

The splash reports that Truss is now the favourite with both bookmakers and Conservative activists, but her allies fear that Sunak supporters might strike 'dirty backroom deals' to keep her off the ballot.

The theme is continued inside on the news spread, where a Jason Groves analysis notes that Sunak's team are masters of the dark arts, in the leader, and by Stephen Glover in his OpEd column. Glover admits there is no proof of any the suspected machinations and insists that he is not making any allegations, but he says it would be a 'despicable act' if Sunak were to advance Part-time Penny's cause in any way. She is so obviously unsuitable to be PM that Sunak would never be forgiven if he helped her into No 10.

There doesn't seem to be a lot of forgiveness available in the Mail for Mr Sunak.

MORDAUNT UNDER THE MICROSCOPE

Penny in trade storm

Row with own staff as she tries to 'take credit' for deal during leadership bid

She turned to Gordon Brown for advice

'Totally inappropriate'

'Cutting up rough in her department'

Blow to leader bid as Ellwood loses whip

Vow to make tech giants pay to use news

I KNOW she's trying to rewrite history on her trans views

COMMENTARY
By Stephanie Davies-Arai

Meanwhile, the attacks on Mordaunt continue on the second news spread. This time it's 'Penny in trade storm' and an allegation that she is trying to rewrite history over her views on gender.

Having rued (yet again) that the contest is taking place at all and dismissed Mordaunt (again) as unsuitable, the leader says the fact that she is still in second place has led to suspicions that the Sunak camp will try to use dirty tricks to scupper the foreign secretary – who is 'building up a formidable head of steam' – in the final ballot.

> *A cynical stitch-up would be an anti-democratic outrage, denying activists a choice between Conservative ideologies.*
>
> *This paper has always argued the last battle should be between Miss Truss and Mr Sunak. Both are experienced politicians. Both have deftly handled daunting Cabinet challenges. But Miss Truss is a low-tax, small-state Tory and Mr Sunak is closer to being a third way liberal.*

21 July

Daily Mail

THURSDAY, JULY 21, 2022 Daily newspaper of the year 80p

LIZ v RISHI: THE BATTLE BEGINS

TRUSS: I'LL HOLD AN EMERGENCY TAX CUT BUDGET

EXCLUSIVE: Writing in the Mail, she vows to build an 'aspiration nation' – and stand up to those who talk down 'our country, history and values'

By Jason Groves and Harriet Line

LIZ Truss today vows to beat Labour by 'governing as a true tax-cutting, freedom-loving Conservative'.

The Foreign Secretary last night surged into the final run-off against Rishi Sunak in the race to become prime minister, knocking out rival Penny Mordaunt.

Writing in the Daily Mail today, Miss Truss sets out an agenda that will see her pursuing Boris Johnson's freedom-loving instincts while reversing Mr Sunak's high-tax agenda.

In an attack on the former chancellor's record, she says the Government has been 'going in the wrong direction on tax, with the tax burden at its highest in 70 years'.

She pledges to hold an emergency budget to push through immediate tax cuts to ease the cost of living and encourage enterprise.

'We cannot have business-as-usual managerialism on the economy,' she writes.

'I am the tax-cutting candidate who will help squeezed families by reversing April's national insurance rise and suspending the green levy on energy bills.'

Miss Truss also promises to take on the 'Whitehall Blob' to

Turn to Page 4

Ballot winner: Rishi Sunak yesterday

Favourite: Liz Truss saw off Penny Mordaunt

We're down to the final two – Liz v Rishi. Mordaunt misses the cut by eight votes. To what extent that was due to the Mail's campaigning for Truss and whether we were denied a more effective prime minister or spared an even greater catastrophe, we shall never know.

The Mail buries the final figures in its exclusive splash: Truss writing for the Mail, promising an emergency budget and expounding on her plans to build an aspiration nation.

Her bylined piece on page 4 promises immediate tax cuts, says that she will stop people 'talking down our great country', and expresses confidence that she will beat Labour at the next election. Further back, there are two spreads: Rishi being mocked for looking out of place in Birmingham, and a comparison of the 'smug head boy' and 'Maggie's sterner sister'.

LIZ v RISHI: THE BATTLE BEGINS

Rishi mingled in terrace bar, as out of place as a rare bird fluttering over streets of Birmingham...

By Jason Groves

THEN THERE WERE TWO

After Prada shoes, it's a £3,500 bespoke suit

Sunak loses time to woo the grassroots in postal votes blow

No let up in scramble for support

LIZ v RISHI: THE BATTLE BEGINS

Slightly smug Head Boy VS Maggie's sterner sister

Irreverent portraits of wannabe PMs by RICHARD KAY and ANDREW PIERCE

Glover likes Truss's policies, but isn't so sure about her presentation; the leader says 'What a relief'. It's got the two candidates it wants, it's up to members of course, but it's clear who the Mail would prefer in No 10.

Week 3

TAX CUTS? YES PLEASE

22 July

Channel migrants are supposedly landing on Kent beaches with guns, Prince George is having a birthday, and Boris Johnson is back in the limelight. It's no surprise then that, now the Mail has its chosen finalists, the leadership contest is reduced to four pages, starting on page 11.

LIZ v RISHI: BATTLE FOR No10

Liz: I'm Labour's worst nightmare

Bullish Truss hits ground running with warning to the doubters

I feared a mud pie would splat on her white jacket at any moment

HENRY DEEDES SKETCH

Sunak accused of rewriting history over lockdown veto

Poll has Liz on 62%, Rishi at 38%

BBC stokes 'Maggie blouse' row

Truss takes centre stage again on the only spread – where it's Sunak's turn to be accused of rewriting history – while the first of two single pages is devoted to the two contenders going head-to-head on tax policy. Truss says Sunak would bring recession, Sunak says Truss would bring higher interest rates. The second has another attack on Mordaunt, even though she's now out of the running.

The leader writers are focused on the economy. And, given the way things panned out, it's quite the read:

> *Make no mistake: Severe economic turbulence awaits whoever becomes Britain's next prime minister. Debt interest payments have hit a record high and monthly government borrowing is at eye-watering levels, fuelled by soaring inflation.*
>
> *The Mail is attracted to Liz Truss's plan to bulldoze the Whitehall 'blob' into immediate tax cuts, intending to boost economic growth and ease the spiralling cost of living. But with the nation's finances creaking so badly, will that be possible?*
>
> *Rishi Sunak, meanwhile, wants to maintain fiscal responsibility - another traditional Tory value (even though he sprayed public money around like there was no tomorrow while chancellor). That would mean delaying tax cuts which could help painfully squeezed families.*
>
> *This is why it is so vital to scrutinise the competing visions of the two candidates as they battle for the keys to No 10 - and not just naively swallow their grand promises. The economic future of Britain is at stake.*

As to Johnson, there is outrage over the parliamentary standards inquiry into whether he misled parliament over lockdown parties* in Downing Street – the 'goalposts have been moved', so that he'll be at fault even if he turns out to have done so unintentionally. This, his supporters say, is a witch-hunt.

Partygate a distraction, Beergate a scandal

Daily Mail

The inconvenient truth about Harry and the Queen

BY RICHARD KAY

Boris's plea as MPs force yet ANOTHER inquiry...

HOW LONG CAN THE PARTYGATE FARCE GO ON?

Two child victims of killers aged just 13 – and yet more grotesque failings

Daily Mail

And the Wagatha winner is... The Mail's Judge Jane delivers her verdict

Boris in clear as Partygate probe is shut down after four months... sparking fury over the Met's warped priorities

WHAT A FARCICAL WASTE OF TIME AND £460,000

KATE'S NEW WINGMAN

**From the word go, the Mail has sought to minimise Partygate and the suitcases-full-of-wine drinking culture that flourished on Johnson's watch. It acknowledged that people who weren't allowed to see dying loved ones while Westminster was partying felt betrayed, but it believed the attention the scandal was getting was disproportionate. It strongly disapproved of the parliamentary standards inquiry (the splash on April 22 was 'How long can the Partygate farce go on?') and of the Metropolitan Police squandering resources on investigating a series of events that led to more than 100 fines.*

After Johnson (and Sunak) received just one penalty notice each for what looked to many the least egregious breach of lockdown rules, the paper's May 20 splash was 'What a farcical waste of time and £460,000'. From then on, the whole scandal was boiled down to 'a cake that never left its Tupperware box'.

Meanwhile, those two 'farce' headlines were bookends for a concerted campaign – eight lead stories in eleven days – to get Durham police to reinvestigate Keir Starmer, who had been filmed (by the son of a former Mail writer) drinking from a beer bottle on a single occasion while out campaigning. 'Starmer the Covid party hypocrite' had made an exclusive splash for the paper back in January; the police had looked into the allegations at the time and taken no action.

Under pressure from the Mail and Tory MPs, they looked again. Starmer was then accused of seeking to influence the investigation by saying that he would resign if found to have broken the law. The Mail, which didn't at all try to influence the police investigation and had already made clear that, in the prime minister's case at least, law-breaking was not a resignation matter, would naturally have been happy for Starmer to continue in office had he been fined.

Daily Mail

Photo test that proves who wears the trousers in YOUR relationship

POLICE REVIEW OVER STARMER'S LOCKDOWN DRINKS

Daily Mail

DAMNING SIX-PAGE DOSSIER

LABOUR'S LOCKDOWN LIES AND HYPOCRISY

Daily Mail

NEW LOOK weekend

The astonishing decline and fall of jailed Becker by RICHARD KAY

After Mail exposes cover-up over 'Beergate' party...

POLICE TOLD TO INVESTIGATE LABOUR'S LIES

I'm standing by him, says wife of Tory MP who watched porn in Commons

ROYAL BIRTHDAY SPECIAL

Daily Mail

Beaming amid the bluebells, Charlotte at seven (with a new best friend)

SHOW US THE PROOF, SIR KEIR

Daily Mail

Same dress, but Kim is just a poundshop replica of Marilyn

SARAH VINE

BEERGATE: DAY 7

MAN WHO JUST CAN'T ANSWER A STRAIGHT QUESTION

WIN

Daily Mail

ALL your bills paid for a year!

Mortgage or rent ++ Groceries ++ Fuel ++ Utilities ++ Health ++ Holidays

BEERGATE: DAY 10

NOW IT'S SLIPPERY STARMER IN CRISIS

Meghan and Harry Jubilee balcony ban

Daily Mail

INSPIRE MAGAZINE

Rough diamond and charmer whose life mirrored the TV rogues we all loved

RATTLED STARMER SNUBS THE CHANCE TO CLEAR AIR

Still Killing it: Jodie's glory night at Baftas

BEERGATE: DAY 11

Daily Mail

The gut guru who could transform your health joins the Mail today

BEERGATE: DAY 13

STARMER ACCUSED OF PILING PRESSURE ON POLICE

Robert Hardman

Is Queen's absence today the first step towards a Charles Regency?

They've bottled it!

... after he piled on the pressure with threat to resign

Boris and Carrie WON'T have wedding party at Chequers

But in the end – after spending 3,200 manhours and £101,000 – the police concluded for the second time that the Labour leader had broken no rules. The Mail headline on this verdict – the day after Johnson quit – was 'They've bottled it'; the intro reported that Starmer had 'escaped a fine', but 'suspicions had been raised that the decision was politically motivated'. The people with those suspicions were Michael Fabricant and a Conservative county councillor.

23 July

Boris is back at the centre of attention on a day of thin gruel from the contenders (Sunak is 'under fire for Covid fraud billions', Truss is promising to 'throw off EU chains').

LIZ v RISHI: BATTLE FOR No10

Sunak under fire for Covid fraud billions

After Liz as Maggie, Rishi does a Dave...

Scan this QR code to vote in our poll on The Mail+

Emergency action is needed to save the NHS from breaking, he warns

Did his video breach rules?

Truss: I'll throw off EU chains by end of next year

Penny's allies 'in revenge plot'

'Deliver on the promise of Brexit'

'A British-style revolution'

Big business backs her vow to cut tax

Saturday Essay

First there are the attempts to stop the Partygate witch-hunt, amid fears that the panel conducting the inquiry has already made up its mind. Then there's Lord Cruddas (who was ennobled by Johnson, having previously been rejected by the honours vetting committee) saying that Tories should be given a chance to say that his resignation should be torn up. At the top of that page, though, party members are warned that spoiling their ballot papers by writing in Johnson would only help Sunak.

And the Mail really doesn't seem to want to help Sunak. Here's Amanda Platell saying she would never vote for such a snake and back-stabber, a man who presented himself as a man of integrity and truth, but was, in fact, 'always out for himself'. She challenges him on his wife's nondom tax status, the campaign website set up last year, and his claim to have prevented another Covid lockdown before concluding:

The truth is Rishi Sunak has been on manoeuvres for months, waiting for the most damaging moment to make his venomous strike.

He is not a man to be trusted. Like many other Tories, I will never vote for a snake like him.

Rishi Sunak went missing. No.10 suspected Gove was on manoeuvres. Party chairman Dowden was first to wield the knife. Based on inside accounts, ANDREW PIERCE reveals in forensic detail…

WHAT THE HELL HAVE THEY DONE?

How Boris was betrayed by a very Tory COUP

Andrew Pierce exposé

Team Boris told him he'd easily survive the no confidence vote

Complacency led to his downfall, as it had to Thatcher's

He had a chance to admit a mistake; fatally, he didn't

There's a further Saturday treat way back on pages 28 and 29, where readers find another Andrew Pierce exposé, this time of how Johnson was 'betrayed in a very Tory coup'. It is, he says, a tale of 'jaw-dropping treachery and duplicitous ministers'. And the first words in the strapline are 'Rishi Sunak'.

If we can't trust him on matters of integrity and loyalty, what about his policies?

Well, Sunak is found wanting here, too, in the eyes of a panel of eight 'experts' asked to run the rule over the two candidates' ideas about the economy. Four back Truss and only two Sunak (Gosh! Who'd have thought it!), while the other two are undecided. The Truss backers include Patrick Minford, the inspiration for Trussonomics. Sunak supporters include Black Wednesday chancellor Norman Lamont.

25 July

Daily Mail

MONDAY, JULY 25, 2022 Daily newspaper of the year 80p

Play thousands of puzzles on your tablet or phone!

PLUS read the paper and so much more with our The Mail+ app

To subscribe for £1 for 3 months visit mailsubscriptions.co.uk

As Rishi attacks Liz over Beijing, her camp hits back...

TOUGH ON CHINA, MR SUNAK? PULL THE OTHER ONE

The contest returns to the front with a Truss camp attack on Sunak over his attitude to China, while the inside spread is split between Truss promising to not to 'cower' to European courts over our borders and a call to 'Bring back Boris'.

26 July

TRUSS VOW TO CURB MILITANT UNIONS

As rivals clash in fiery TV debate that can only have cheered Labour, Liz unveils blueprint to stop strikers crippling UK

By Harriet Line and David Churchill

LIZ Truss vowed last night to stop militant trade unions trying to 'paralyse' the economy.

Turn to Page 4

Truss 'won't let Whitehall blob block £30bn tax cuts'

She'll have final say, Cabinet ally vows as experts back her plans

'Stimulating growth has to be the foundation'

£4.50 EARRINGS

£3,500 SUIT

Nadine gives Sunak a dressing-down over £3,500 suit

Tory voters: Sorry Rishi, we want Liz

Another TV debate keeps the story on page 1, and Truss gets the splash again, vowing to curb militant unions.

Inside, a spread accuses Sunak of a new Project Fear, while Truss has a page lead on countering the 'Whitehall blob'. Nadine Dorries weighs in to criticise Sunak's expensive suits and praise Truss's economy earrings. The leader applauds Truss for her pledge to 'take on the wreckers'.

LIZ v RISHI: BATTLE FOR No10

Now Rishi accused of peddling Project Fear

Bad-tempered TV debate sees Truss hit back over tax claim

Sunak jabbered furiously like a man who'd washed down Pro Plus with a treble espresso

HENRY DEEDES SKETCH

27 July

The race moves back in the book, with Sunak changing tack on energy bills Truss saying she'll make police investigate real crimes, not Twitter rows. The big news is TalkTV's Kate McCann fainting while hosting the latest debate and Truss first being aghast and then rushing to her aid.

LIZ v RISHI: BATTLE FOR No10

Sunak in £4billion energy bills U-turn

He lines up eye-catching policy pledge... but as chancellor he'd blocked Boris's plan to do same

HENRY DEEDES SKETCH

Oh my God, cried Liz as the host swooned. It was drama, just not the sort they wanted

The leader bemoans a lack of boosterism and urges both candidates to paint a more positive picture.

> *Miss Truss's plan to turbocharge* the struggling economy with immediate tax cuts if she becomes prime minister is right... Whoever wins the Tory race can drag Britain out of the economic mire by unshackling dynamic businesses in cutting edge sectors - and not selling them off to the highest foreign bidder. That, and channelling Boris's positivity, can help beat Labour.*

[With more than a dozen appearances in four months, 'turbocharging' the struggling/stagnant economy and/or growth is another one for the Mail leader bingo card.]

28 July

LIZ v RISHI: BATTLE FOR No10

Rivals launch crime crusade for women

RISHI: I'll curb the grooming gangs – and give women freedom to go out at night without fear

'I will introduce a major crackdown'

By Rishi Sunak

Sexual violence against women and girls should be treated as a national emergency until it's been defeated

LIZ: I'll turn the relentless tide of public sexual comments and bring in a law against 'street harassment'

Boost Commonwealth 'to counter China trade threat'

Sunak at last gets a byline. But, unlike Truss's efforts for the paper, his offering does not make a splash or a front-page puff. Indeed, his assertion that sexual violence against women is a national emergency is not even the main headline for the day's leadership coverage – way back on pages 14 and 15.

That proclaims 'Rivals launch crime crusade for women', with the two agendas given a page each. Liz and her promise of a law against street harassment is on the right – always the first one readers look at – with two pictures. The main one has her in the centre of a crowd of young people waving Liz for Leader placards, while a drop-in has her open-mouthed and waving.

White-shirted Rishi is also open-mouthed with hands aloft in a small photograph on the left, where the page lead gives readers a precis of what they can read if they look at the piece immediately below.

Week 4

BRUTUS BEGONE! WE LOVE LOYAL LIZ

29 July

The first public hustings in Leeds bring Sunak a rare top-billing in the day's muted coverage of the contest, with a page 10 pledge to make it easier to establish new grammar schools.

Truss, having promised on page 2 to be Ukraine's friend, is on home territory for the 'leadership' coverage on page 10, promising to harness the 'gritty spirit' of former Leeds United manager Don Revie*.

30 July

After a quiet couple of days, another TV debate is covered with another inside spread. This time the verdict is that Sunak has been 'mauled over tax record' and there is a sketch describing how he 'sat awkwardly like a man waiting for an enema'. He is also accused by defence secretary Ben Wallace of blocking defence spending. Wallace has come out for Truss. She, meanwhile, has won over the 'Turnip Taliban' after '13 tough years'. These are apparently people in her Norfolk constituency who don't care for her.

LIZ v RISHI: BATTLE FOR No10

Rishi's mauled over tax record

In a bruising TV encounter, he denies his policies will hit economy

HENRY DEEDES SKETCH

The ex-Chancellor sat awkwardly, like a man about to undergo an enema

After 13 tough years, Liz finally wins over the 'Turnip Taliban'

Sunak blocked defence spending, says Wallace as he supports 'honest' Truss

He vows to take on woke brigade

The leader picks up Truss's references to Don Revie at the Leeds hustings and says she is growing into her campaign:

> *Her economic priorities are immediate tax cuts to stimulate growth, suspension of green levies and a bonfire of stifling regulation - music to the ears of many Tories...*
>
> *Drawing on her Yorkshire upbringing, she says she has been channelling the spirit of the great Leeds United manager Don Revie*. He embodied hard graft, self-belief and an unshakeable determination to win. Essential qualities in a football manger. Even more essential in a prime minister.*

**Don Revie was an enormously successful manager and earned the respect and loyalty of many, although his team's footballing style had detractors and they were nicknamed 'dirty Leeds'. Revie was the obvious choice to succeed Alf Ramsey as England manager (after a period under caretaker Joe Mercer), but his spell in charge was hardly smooth.*

Eventually, in an exclusive article for the Mail, he revealed that he intended to resign and take up a lucrative contract with the United Arab Emirates. His reputed affection for money earned him the sobriquet Don Readies and there were unproven claims of financial impropriety. After his resignation, and in the wake of bribery allegations, the FA suspended him for ten years for bringing the game into disrepute. Revie took the case to court and the suspension was overturned, but Mr Justice Cantley described him as greedy and prickly, and said his resignation had shown a 'sensational, outrageous example of disloyalty, breach of trust, discourtesy and selfishness'.

The judge could have had a career as a Mail leader writer.

1 August

The Lionesses' Euros triumph dominates, but the leadership contest makes a spread on 10 and 11, with Truss promising to free farmers from red tape and Sunak revealing a 'radical' tax cut in a 'last bid to win votes'.

LIZ v RISHI: BATTLE FOR No10

Truss: We'll free our farmers of red tape

Sweeping plans to feed Britain will scythe through outdated EU rules

Getting out? Never.

Rishi reveals 'radical' tax cut in last bid to win votes

Nadine accused over 'stab in the back' Sunak image

My creeping sense of panic, by fainting TV host

The leader applauds Truss for helping to fend off a 'food apocalypse' and has kind words, too, for Sunak on plans to fine patients who miss NHS appointments. Both show that they are far superior to the cowardly and 'achingly metropolitan' Starmer who might 'struggle to identify basic farmyard animals'.

2 August

Daily Mail

TUESDAY, AUGUST 2, 2022 | Daily newspaper of the year | 80p

'In an age where women's very existence is being denied, this glorious show of bold femininity can change the world'

BY JULIE BURCHILL

Warrior queen: Chloe Kelly celebrates with team mates after scoring the winner at Wembley

LIZ: I'LL HALT JUNK FOOD TAX

By John Stevens Deputy Political Editor

LIZ Truss last night vowed to call a halt on taxes aimed at deterring families from buying junk food.

The Tory leadership frontrunner said she would scrap proposals for a ban on 'buy one, get one free' deals

Turn to Page 4

As Mordaunt backs leadership bid, Truss tells Mail she'll rip up nanny state plans to ban unhealthy 'buy one, get one free' offers

The ballot papers have gone out to Conservative party members and Truss has given an interview to the Mail – this time about obesity legislation – which provides another splash. The sub-head and inside spread inform readers that Mordaunt is now in Camp Liz. This, after everything the Mail has said about 'Part-time Penny' is presented as a 'major coup'. Former Spice Girl Geri Halliwell also tells us what she wants, what she really, really wants: 'Lizzie' to win.

LIZ v RISHI: BATTLE FOR No10

Penny's now in the Truss camp

Major coup for leadership frontrunner as third-placed Mordaunt supports former rival

Geri: I really, really, really want Lizzie in power!

Rishi under fire for 'mañana' tax cuts instead of help for families

Back 'rational' Sunak, Hague urges Tory members

A small story at the bottom of the spread has William Hague urging members to vote Sunak.

The leader celebrates Truss's boosterism, comparing her promise of immediate tax cuts with Sunak's talk of 4p off the basic rate of income tax by the end of the next parliament – 'if a week is a long time in politics, seven years is a geological epoch'.

Truss, it says, is growing steadily stronger and clearly relishing the husting. And don't forget she was loyal – unlike others we could mention.

> *Miss Truss has already proved as Foreign Secretary both her steadfast support for Ukraine in the face of Vladimir Putin's barbarism and her determination to stand equally firm against EU bullying over the Northern Ireland Protocol.*
>
> *With each passing day, more senior Tories are declaring their support for Miss Truss - most recently former leadership contenders Penny Mordaunt and Nadhim Zahawi.*
>
> *A Boris Johnson loyalist to the end, Miss Truss is mapping out a 'boosterist' agenda to take forward his legacy. It is clearly resonating with the parliamentary party and the grassroots membership.*

3 August

Daily Mail

WEDNESDAY, AUGUST 3, 2022 Daily newspaper of the year 80p

She has the boldness, vision and strength of conviction to build on what Boris began. That's why today the Mail backs Liz Truss for leader

Daily Mail COMMENT PAGE 19

We've known where the Mail was heading all along and now it comes out and says it in a top-of-the-front blue panel and full-page leader: 'the Mail backs Truss'.

The endorsement comes the day after Truss performs the first of her many U-turns, backing away from a suggestion that regional pay boards should be established so that public sector workers in the North would end up being paid less than those in the South. This is presented as a 'despite' bit of a report on her growing poll lead.

LIZ v RISHI: BATTLE FOR No10

Truss ready to end jail threat over TV licences

I'm very concerned about how many women have been locked up, she says

Daily Mail COMMENT

£500m bill to taxpayers as firms given Rishi's Covid loans go bust

Fraud unit finally set to hunt down lost millions

Liz extends her poll lead despite public pay U-turn furore

Sunak: I'll treat anyone who 'vilifies' UK as extremists just like terrorists

The main story from the campaign is her pledge to lift the threat of jail over people who do not pay their TV licence. The story reports that three-quarters of the 114,000 people convicted of licence dodging in 2019 were women and that Truss was 'alarmed at the number of women being locked up'. It does not report that you cannot be jailed for not having a licence – only for contempt if you refuse to pay the resultant fine. Two people have been jailed over this since 2019.

But the big news for the Mail is its verdict that Truss should be prime minister – although it must first remind everyone that the election shouldn't be taking place, Boris should still be in power. On every issue that truly mattered, he had made the right calls at the right time. He delivered a Brexit deal against all the odds, guided the country through the worst pandemic in a century and facilitated a vaccine miracle, and he 'galvanised the world' against the barbarous Vladimir Putin.

He would have recovered from a 'disproportionate hate campaign' over 'a confection of relatively trivial* matters' and gone on to win another election. But his colleagues forgot the meaning of loyalty and allowed themselves to be brainwashed by a combination of malign Twitterati, squealing Remainers, a relentlessly hostile broadcast media and a contemptible fifth column within his parliamentary party.

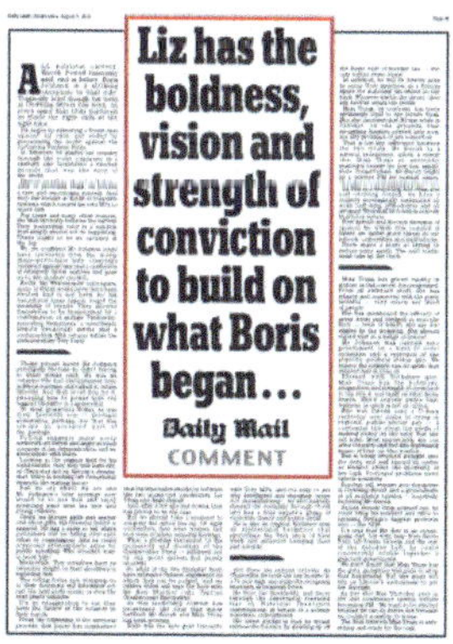
Liz has the boldness, vision and strength of conviction to build on what Boris began…

Daily Mail
COMMENT

But Boris has gone and we are where we are; the final two are worthy candidates and either – here comes that Johnson soundbite again – would 'wipe the floor with Sir Keir Starmer (aka Captain Crasheroonie Snoozefest)'.

Trivial misdemeanours . . .

**The only 'trivial' lapses the Mail refers to in the period after Johnson's resignation are Partygate and the 'deeply undedifying Chris Pincher sex pest affair'. Others may feel there were more, such as lying to the Queen about the need to prorogue parliament to stifle Brexit debate and trying to change Commons rules to spare his friend Owen Paterson.*

Even the two the Mail mentions are not generally seen as trivial. It is right that people weren't that upset about the birthday cake, but they were appalled by the partying the night before the Duke of Edinburgh's funeral, where the Queen was pictured sitting alone in the choir at St George's Chapel, obeying the rules that those who set them flouted.

The Mail ON SUNDAY

£5 OFF AT HOUSE OF FRASER
When you spend £25 or more
COUPON PAGE 44

FREE £5 MARKS & SPENCER GIFT CARD

No10 fears another by-election as we reveal Boris joked about 'handsy' MP before giving him top Government job

PM KNEW ALL ABOUT 'GROPING' TORY TWO YEARS AGO

EXCLUSIVE

PICTURE EXCLUSIVE
Dapper Rupert seen for first time since split with Jerry
SEE PAGE 5

Nor was Pincher just an unedifying 'sex pest affair'. Pincher resigned as deputy chief whip after being accused of groping two men while drunk. But the groping wasn't the issue. The scandal – the one that would bring down the prime minister – was that Johnson had known for two years about Pincher's reputation for 'being handsy' (he himself quipped 'Pincher by name, pincher by nature') and had been warned against appointing him to an office responsible for discipline. This was reported as an 'exclusive' by the Mail's Sunday sister on July 3, blowing the story wide open, since not only had Johnson denied receiving such a warning, but ministers had been sent out on the media round to repeat the denial. As ever, it wasn't the sex scandal that was fatal, but the cover-up and lying (the Mail calls it dissembling) afterwards. Sajid Javid and Rishi Sunak decided enough was enough and quit, starting the resignation avalanche that did for Johnson.

. . and heroic successes

The Mail also picks out the same three 'successes': delivering Brexit, the Covid vaccine, Ukraine.

Brexit: both Johnson and his chief negotiator Lord Frost subsequently denounced the deal they had agreed. The Northern Ireland protocol is still not working: we are in dispute with the EU over it and the DUP is so angry about it as it stands that it has boycotted Stormont, leaving the province without a government for months and the prospect of an unwanted election. The 'migrant crisis' that would disappear once we had the right to 'control our borders' is still headline news. These are just the most visible pieces of evidence that Brexit is not yet 'done'. Remoaners would cite many more.

Covid furlough and the vaccine miracle: the former was down to Sunak, the latter to scientists, Kate Bingham's roll-out team and the NHS. No mention is made – now – of the missed Cobra meetings, the care home deaths, the failings of the £37bn test-and-trace project, the £4.3bn loans fraud or the £8.7bn wasted on useless PPE. The Mail was strident in reporting all of these (apart from the Cobra meetings) and was one of the first to raise the alarm about care homes.

It reminds readers that Johnson almost died from the virus, but declines to hold him in any way responsible for the tens of thousands who did succumb; on the contrary, he is credited with 'saving thousands of lives'.

Measurable successes are down to him, expensive failings blamed on others. Yes, the vaccine was developed and distributed on his watch – but if he is applauded for that achievement, how can he be exculpated for the lockdown breaches that took place not only on his watch, but under his own roof?

Ukraine: Johnson has been praised internationally for his steadfastness. But there is no reason to believe that any other leader would have been less staunch.

Back to that leader, the Mail first addresses Sunak:

> *Rishi was the ante-post favourite with Tory MPs, and it's easy to see why. Intelligent and engaging (when not mansplaining), he successfully steered the economy through Covid and has a true expert's grasp of economic theory and policy detail.*
>
> *He is also an original Brexiteer with an aspirational back story that epitomises the Tory ideal of hard work and initiative bringing their just rewards.*
>
> *But there are serious caveats. As Chancellor, he took the tax burden to a 70-year high and supports swingeing increases in business levies. He froze tax thresholds, and drove through the universally resented rise in National Insurance contributions, in breach of a solemn manifesto commitment.*
>
> *His latest pledge is that he would redress the balance by slashing 4p off the basic rate of income tax - but only within seven years!*
>
> *In addition, he will be forever seen by many Tory members as a Brutus figure for stabbing his friend in the back. Whoever wields the sword, they say, seldom wears the crown.*

Truss, on the other hand, had been unfailingly loyal to her former boss and opposed the NI rise on the grounds that struggling families needed help now, not airy promises of jam tomorrow.

She had grown visibly in stature during the contest after an awkward start, relaxing and connecting to the party faithful – 'her kind of people'. While Sunak was a natural technocrat, Truss was an authentic standard-bearer for low-tax, small-state Conservatism.

Blessed with Yorkshire grit, Miss Truss has the boldness, imagination and strength of conviction to tap into it and build on what Boris began...Most importantly, she can unite the party and end this depressing spasm of blue-on-blue warfare...

Success will require iron discipline in Downing Street and a government of all available talents – hopefully including Mr Sunak.'

The 'ocean-going dud' Starmer could cobble together a 'gimcrack government' with the LibDems, SNP, Greens and the rest of the deluded Left, but

We don't doubt Miss Truss has the guts, gumption and guile to stop that happening...the Mail believes Miss Truss is able, willing and ready for the task.

4 August

LIZ v RISHI: BATTLE FOR No10

Now Javid turns on ex-ally Rishi and endorses Truss

Sunak 'hindered by role in PM betrayal'

As she vows to tackle ambulance delays

By Dan Hodges

THE WAY THEY WERE...

With shape shifting new friends like The Saj, Liz should beware

A quiet day. Sajid Javid changes camps to line up behind Truss and, with the Bank of England about to raise interest rates again, Alex Brummer says that all the doom and gloom about the economy is misplaced...

Week 5

TRUSS LOOKS A SHOE-IN

5 August

Daily Mail

FRIDAY, AUGUST 5, 2022 | Daily newspaper of the year | 80p

PREMIER LEAGUE

The best signings. Club-by-club guide

Your 12-page guide to Premier League

It's back tonight!

Why City are WEAKER now!

Inflation's set to hit almost SEVEN times his official target.

Critics accuse Bank Governor of being asleep at the wheel.

Now we face a YEAR of recession – and soaring interest rates

BANKER WHO'S RUNNING OUT OF CREDIT

Deflation: Bank of England Governor Andrew Bailey yesterday

By Lucy White
Chief City Reporter

THE Bank of England faced a ferocious backlash last night after admitting inflation will pass 13 per cent.

Bank Governor Andrew Bailey was forced to deny he had been 'asleep at the wheel' as he warned that Britain faced a lengthy recession.

Critics said Bank officials should 'rue the day' they decided not to raise interest rates last year. It came as grim economic predictions forced the Bank to raise interest rates by 0.5 percentage points – the largest amount since 1995 – to reach 1.75 per cent.

It is a highly unusual move. While higher rates can help to tame prices, they can also slam the brakes on economic growth.

The Bank also revised its expectations for inflation to a peak of 13.3 per cent in October. Just two months ago, it was predicting a maximum of 11 per cent.

The Bank said the red-hot inflation will cause the UK to slump into a

Turn to Page 4

...but if there is a problem – such as a mortgage time bomb for millions – it's all the fault of Andrew Bailey for not putting up interest rates earlier. The Governor is running out of credit and Truss will review the Bank of England's independence.

She also says there doesn't have to be a recession and she is now 'shimmying' on set for her appearance in the final TV debate. In this she is going 'face-to-face' with Sunak, but there is no sign of him on the page. The photograph is of Truss sitting down with Kay Burley, both in red dresses and high heels.

Page 10 Daily Mail, Friday, August 5, 2022

There doesn't HAVE to be a recession, says Truss

By Martin Beckford, John Stevens and Georgia Edkins

LIZ Truss insisted that a recession was not inevitable last night as the Tory leadership candidates' plans for the economy came under close scrutiny.

In the very first question of a live Tory leadership debate on Sky News, the frontrunner was asked what she could do to lessen the impact of the looming slowdown.

Ladies in red: Liz Truss is quizzed by Kay Burley

'We can change the outcome'

Liz's joints have loosened up and she shimmied around the stage

HENRY DEEDES SKETCH

Rishi's housing pledge to bring in young voters

6 August

COST OF LIVING CRUNCH

You're far too gloomy, Bank chief is warned

Beleaguered Governor slammed for 'adding to sense of panic' following doom-laden UK forecast

House prices start to dip

Truss: I'll do everything I can to help struggling families

Household bills 'to rise by £6,000' this winter

Will Kwarteng be Liz's chancellor?

Electricity theft hits new high as fuel prices soar

Business leaders and economists agree that the Bank of England is far too gloomy. Truss promises to do everything she can to help struggling families, while Sunak puts his foot in it by telling people in Tunbridge Wells that he had diverted funds from deprived areas.

Andrew Neil says the Left believes that Truss is 'inexperienced, inconsistent, unimpressive, ill-informed, accident-prone, with a weak grasp of the facts and leaden in action, whether under attack or on the offensive'.

He adds: 'The Left is not entirely wrong.'

Neil believes that it is not Starmer's Left that Truss has to worry about:

> *It is what is best described as the Left Blob, which is now omnipresent in British public life, dominant in the citadels of power, including most of the media (above all the broadcasters), the Civil Service, the NHS, the legal system (including the judiciary), education (especially the universities), social media, most public bodies and private charities. It's even wheedling its way into boardrooms.*

Warming to his theme (which could have been the template for Truss's anti-growth coalition riff at the party conference), he continues:

Truss has no idea what is about to be unleashed on her. Constant and vitriolic assaults on social media, especially by the deranged Twitterati, to rouse the mob.

ANDREW NEIL

Truss's biggest foe won't be Starmer but the entire Left Blob who will wage a vitriolic campaign to destroy her

There is a chance it will all unravel before winter is out and the Tories will be back in another contest

A daily pounding on broadcast news, which has already largely decided it hates her. Relentless snide comments on BBC 'comedy' shows. Subtle put-downs from the panjandrums of grand public bodies. Not-so-subtle put downs from our cultural tsars.

In all this, The Blob will be assisted by Remain Tory grandees like John Major and Michael Heseltine who've already concluded she's a wrong 'un. Even Dominic Cummings, fresh from his (almost certain) failure to install Rishi Sunak as prime minister, will likely get in on the act.

Truss is vulnerable because she makes too many mistakes, too many U-turns and offers too many hostages to fortune. So she will need the strongest of chiefs of staff in Downing Street, one with experience and authority, to impose order on the Truss operation – but also to take her aside and tell her when she's about to make a mistake.

And, showing a prescience not evident in the leader four days earlier, he concludes:

It's a tall order. It's not clear she has it in her to do it. There is a chance it will all unravel before winter is out and the Tories would be back in yet another leadership contest, which will stretch voters' patience to breaking point.

8 August

Daily Mail

MONDAY, AUGUST 8, 2022 | Daily newspaper of the year | 90p | 55p to subscribers*

AMAZING NEWSPAPER OFFER

Want your Daily Mail FOR ONLY 55p?

We're rolling back our prices to 2012 when you become a print subscriber

SEE PAGE FOUR FOR DETAILS

PLUS get a £15 M&S gift card* when you subscribe at mailsubs.co.uk/rollback

TORIES 'MUST QUIT BORIS WITCH-HUNT'

Minister tells MPs to resign from 'rigged' Partygate probe

With Truss firmly ahead, the leadership contest takes a back seat to the Mail's efforts to get the inquiry (kangaroo court) into whether Boris Johnson misled Parliament over Downing Street parties halted.

Boris facing 'kangaroo court'

Four Tory MPs who'll help pass judgment on PM

The grandee

The magistrate

The solicitor

The Rishi supporter

He's done nothing to warrant shameful stitch-up

COMMENTARY by Daniel Johnson

'This has more in common with the witch-hunts of Salem'

'Voters will be unforgiving if Boris is thrown under a bus'

But there's still a spread on her promising to scrap the National Insurance increase the moment she moves into No 10. She is, again, the main photograph on the spread – a full-length shot of her looking purposeful as she addresses the faithful – while Sunak is again merely a drop-in, looking intense in ubiquitous white shirt.

LIZ v RISHI: BATTLE FOR No10

Liz: I'll scrap Rishi's tax hike as soon as I am PM

...but both No10 hopefuls criticised for not doing enough about cost of living

By John Stevens
Deputy Political Editor

'Emergency measures'

Trailing: Rishi Sunak

ANDREW PIERCE IS AWAY

75,000 say they won't pay winter energy bills

'Crisis demands a different response'

Lean times ahead! Families cut out meat to save money

10 August

Truss hits out at Rishi doomsters

Our best days are ahead, she says after Raab 'poll suicide' jibe

We need a leader with a bold vision like hers

By Michelle Donelan
Former Tory minister

Live on TV, Liz will answer questions from Mail readers

Now make your voice heard

Quit race now, ex-Army chief tells Sunak

After a day off to focus on Johnson's kangaroo court, the leadership contest is back with a half-hearted spread on which Truss has another pop at the Sunak 'doomsters' and five-minute-wonder education secretary Michelle Donelan says the Tories need a leader with Truss's bold vision. Donelan went on to be appointed culture secretary the following month.

On the OpEd, Stephen Glover has seen enough. Truss is going to win, and win handsomely. It's time for Sunak to step aside so that she can get on with the job – 'We need a functioning PM and we need her now.'

Former army chief Lord Dannatt agrees. Dannatt, 'speaking to the Mail' says: 'It's far better for Rishi to quit and maintain himself as a credible politician, than being thoroughly trounced and be a figure of ridicule.'

It is not immediately apparent quite why the general's opinion on this should be relevant – so relevant as to constitute one of only two news stories on the spread (the final element being a puff for a GB News television interview in which Mail readers will have the opportunity to quiz Liz). He is not a figure renowned for insightful political pronouncements and, as a cross-bench peer, is presumably not a Tory party member. So he does not even have a vote.

11 August

Truss wows her audience in a 'laid-back' chat with GB News at a Greater Manchester working men's club, where she promises to 'use British law' to send asylum seekers to Rwanda. There are four photographs of her looking animated, and an admiring sketch by Henry Deedes (though who knows how flattering the lady in blue would find it to be compared with a 'wizened football manager').

LIZ v RISHI: BATTLE FOR No10

Truss: I'll use British law to protect the Rwanda plan

Bid to stop attempts by Euro court judges to thwart deportation flights

Rishi 'is facing exodus of backers to his rival'

'We'll legislate for Britain'

La Truss was as calm as a wizened football coach talking tactics in the boot room

HENRY DEEDES SKETCH

I'd prefer to lose the race than win on a false promise, admits Rishi

Is there a hole in his budget?

Earlier in the book there is speculation that she might take the pain out of energy bills by cutting VAT.

The paper is hardly bothering to report anything Sunak says now, as the race looks over and done with. He is facing an 'exodus' of backers to his rival, but he says he'd rather lose than win on a false promise. He also has a hole in his shoe.

Week 6

SNEERS, JEERS AT SUNAK

12 August

Just the one page today, conforming to the emerging pattern: Liz good, Sunak bad. In this case former contender Kemi Badenoch says that 'Maverick' Truss's unpredictability is an asset, while two of her supporters accuse Sunak of blocking reforms to cut EU red tape.

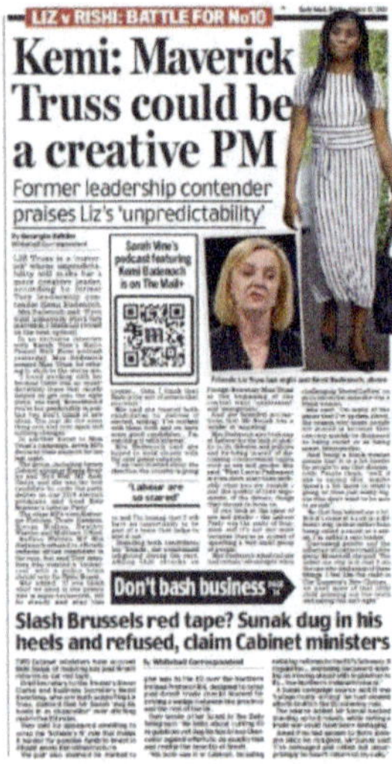
LIZ v RISHI: BATTLE FOR No10

Kemi: Maverick Truss could be a creative PM

Former leadership contender praises Liz's 'unpredictability'

Don't bash business

Slash Brussels red tape? Sunak dug in his heels and refused, claim Cabinet ministers

Liz: I'll end Whitehall wokeism over Israel

Labour braces for 'nightmare'

'Culture that strays into anti-Semitism'

13 August

Another thin day: an inside page lead, with picture, tells us that Truss will 'end Whitehall wokeism over Israel' as part of a 'wider fight against anti-semitism'. Sunak doesn't get a mention at all.

15 August

The leadership race is subsumed into an energy crisis spread that majors on Keir Starmer being wrong. 'Senior Tories' – in this case John Redwood – say his policy of freezing the cap on energy bills for the winter is 'pure socialism that would lead to higher taxes'. Truss's first act in office would be to freeze the cap on energy bills for two years.

Keir's plan 'would make crisis worse'

Truss allies warn vow to freeze cap on energy bills is 'pure socialism' ... and would lead to higher taxes

You could be missing out on an average of £3,300 per year plus other support with Pension Credit

Check your eligibility at gov.uk/pension-credit or by calling 0800 99 1234

'Magical solution to wish it all away'

Now £400 discount may be cut for rich

Liz could revive petrol voucher scheme that was 'blocked by Rishi'

'He only likes ideas he thinks of himself'

£12m for heat and light in empty Whitehall offices

The second story, on the right-hand side, speculates that Truss 'could' revive a petrol voucher scheme reportedly rejected by Sunak (she didn't). The cross-head in the story is 'He only likes ideas he thinks of himself' and is illustrated with that budget picture of Sunak filling up a stranger's car, captioned: 'Backfire: Rishi Sunak fills up a Kia Rio in a much-mocked photo-opportunity'. This is a go-to picture for the Mail and was the one it chose when listing the potential runners and riders to succeed Johnson back in July.

16 August

Page 6 Daily Mail, Tuesday, August 16, 2022

Now another top Tory defects to Truss camp

Frontrunner: Liz Truss winning over Conservatives at a hustings in Cheltenham, Gloucestershire

By **John Stevens**
Deputy Political Editor

A THIRD Conservative MP has publicly switched from supporting Rishi Sunak to Liz Truss in the Tory leadership race.

Writing for The Mail+, former Welsh Secretary Alun Cairns said he believed the Foreign Secretary is best placed to save the Union between England and the rest of the UK.

His defection provides a fresh boost for Miss Truss as the candidates prepare to take part in hustings in Scotland and Northern Ireland this week.

With just three weeks until the next prime minister is announced, she is the runaway favourite after building a commanding lead in opinion polls of Tory members. Mr Cairns' decision to change sides will be seen as further confirmation that Miss Truss is on course to win.

He wrote: 'At the outset of the campaign, I met Rishi Sunak to discuss the future of the Union and was content with his responses. I chose to support him. However, as the campaign has developed, the risks to our Union have become more apparent. There is a need to break out of the current orthodoxy. The future of our Union depends on it.

'For this reason, I have concluded that with the positive ambition for our country and imagination she has shown, alongside her strong track record as a reformer, Liz Truss is best placed to secure our Union.'

Mr Cairns said he had seen Miss Truss reform three Whitehall departments 'impressively'. He added: 'Reforming the culture across the whole of Whitehall to improve outcomes in all nations will be a greater challenge – but the prize of a stable and united Union will be worth it.

'With Liz, we will succeed and celebrate as one country.'

Miss Truss and Mr Sunak will take part in a hustings in Perth today before heading to Belfast tomorrow.

The defection of Mr Cairns – who served as Welsh Secretary for three years under David Cameron, Theresa May and Boris Johnson – comes days after Sir Robert Buckland announced he was no longer endorsing Mr Sunak.

The current Welsh Secretary became the first Cabinet minister to publicly switch his support, writing in the Daily Telegraph that he had changed his mind over the course of the leadership campaign.

Ex-universities minister Chris Skidmore has also defected. It came as veteran Brexiteer Sir Bill Cash announced he would be supporting Miss Truss.

The MP for Stone, who is chairman of the Commons European scrutiny committee, tweeted: 'Being a real Brexiteer for sovereignty, democracy and self-government, I have voted for Liz Truss. She has led from the front on Ukraine, repeal of EU law, saving Northern Ireland and real policies for economic growth.'

Last night Miss Truss launched a fresh attack on Nicola Sturgeon. Writing in the Scottish Daily Mail, she vowed to 'take on' Scotland's First Minister who she said was 'increasingly out of touch'.

■ VOTERS believe Liz Truss would be a better prime minister than Sir Keir Starmer, a poll has shown.

The Redfield and Wilton survey found that 41 per cent would prefer to see the Foreign Secretary in No 10, with 37 per cent choosing the Labour leader.

But Sir Keir was seen as more popular than her leadership rival Rishi Sunak, according to the poll of 2,000 people. Some 41 per cent backed Sir Keir compared with just 34 per cent who chose the ex-chancellor.

A separate Opinium poll of Tory members gave Miss Truss a 22-point lead over Mr Sunak – putting her on 61 per cent.

With ambition and imagination, Liz is best placed to secure our Union

COMMENTARY
by **Alun Cairns MP**
EX-SECRETARY OF STATE FOR WALES

THE challenges facing our next prime minister have been well documented: Energy and food price rises, the resultant inflation, predictions by some of a recession, and conflict in Europe amongst many others.

For me, however, the maintenance of the Union of the United Kingdom must be central to our new leader's thinking and at the heart of the solutions.

As the hustings move to Scotland and Northern Ireland these matters come to the fore.

Since 1998 we have experienced greater divisions between our family of nations and have spent too little time reminding ourselves of the strength of our Union. We need to celebrate our history and culture, recognising the things we have achieved together and the great future we hold – together.

Devolution has created an environment that has facilitated separation, rather than support our common interests. Leading figures in Edinburgh and Cardiff Bay have taken different decisions for the sake of being different.

The whole machinery of government has been focused on pleasing politicians in devolved parliaments. The next prime minister needs to act with imagination in the interests of people living in the nations and for the whole of the United Kingdom.

Having served as Secretary of State for Wales under three different prime ministers, I am more than familiar with the 'devolve and forget' mentality and with the scale of the challenge to reshape thinking.

Whitehall needs to support our Union, rather than undermine it. The scale of this challenge should not be underestimated.

Unless we act, we are heading for a federal state at best or separate nations at worst.

At the outset of the campaign, I met Rishi Sunak to discuss the future of the Union and was content with his responses. I chose to support him.

However, as the campaign has developed, the risks to our Union have become more apparent. There is a need to break out of the current orthodoxy. The future of our Union depends on it.

For this reason, I have concluded that with the positive ambition for our country and imagination she has shown, alongside her strong track record as a reformer, Liz Truss is best placed to secure our Union.

DURING my time in Cabinet, I have seen her reform three separate departments impressively – always focused on improving outcomes.

Reforming the culture across the whole of Whitehall to improve outcomes in all nations will be a greater challenge – but the prize of a stable and united Union will be worth it.

With Liz, we will succeed and celebrate as one country.

Rishi: Civil servants must quit Whitehall for at least a year

By **Kumail Jaffer**
Political Reporter

SENIOR civil servants would need to spend at least a year outside Whitehall under radical reforms pledged by Rishi Sunak.

The former chancellor, who promised the shake-up to 'get Government delivering' again, last night said the plans would tackle Whitehall 'groupthink' and help departments understand business.

In a bid to streamline the civil service, Mr Sunak also said workers will no longer receive pay rises based on how long they have served, but be judged on performance. He said: 'As chancellor I saw parts of the British civil service at its best, delivering world-class Covid support schemes in record time. But the bloated post-Covid state is in need of a shake-up, so I will create a sharper, leaner civil service.

'I'll press ahead with cuts to back office civil service headcount, recruiting and retaining the brightest and best. I'll strengthen civil servants' experience beyond Whitehall, allow Ministers to bring in more external expertise, and bring in performance pay so we have a truly Rolls-Royce service.'

In March the Treasury launched an 'efficiency crackdown' to slash £5.5billion of spending across Whitehall. In December Mr Sunak drew up plans to cut thousands of civil service jobs in London over three years, also calling for an improved Civil Service Fast Stream – suspended for at least a year from 2023 – where trainees gain experience outside of London.

The civil service ballooned by 10 per cent in 2021 with most new roles in London, despite the Government's levelling-up agenda to move jobs out of the capital.

As chancellor, Mr Sunak pledged to move 22,000 roles out of London, though a report by the Onward think tank this year suggested 'efforts to decentralise the civil service are going backwards'.

Another 'top Tory' defects to Truss. This is Alun Cairns, who was Welsh Secretary until his resignation in 2019 over an aide accused of sabotaging a rape trial. Cairns reportedly knew about the aide's role in the case when he endorsed him as a parliamentary candidate, but was subsequently cleared of breaching the ministerial code. Today's coverage has a story about Cairns writing for the Mail about his decision to switch from Sunak to Truss. This is immediately above Cairns's bylined explanation of his decision to switch from Sunak to Truss.

17 August

The new paparazzi
The stars calling the shots

Can you really ward off Alzheimer's?

The Guardian

Truss condemns British workers for lack of 'graft'

Kyiv vows to sow 'chaos' in Russian supply lines

TRUSTED TO DELIVER

Roaring back? Genetics lab aims to let Tasmanian tiger live again

THE TIMES

Is your shirt XXL? The return of the big classic

Oxbridge? No, it's all about the Ivy League now

Police will be sacked for abusing women under tighter rules

Sunak turns on rival over 'moral' duty to ease bills

Saddle cyclists with speed limits too, says minister

The Guardian has an exclusive splash on Truss saying British workers lack the skill and application of foreign rivals and need 'more graft'. The story comes from a leaked tape from her days as chief secretary to the Treasury, and has echoes of a passage in a book she co-authored in 2012 describing British workers as 'idlers'. She has since said that Sunak-supporting Dominic Raab wrote that particular chapter.

The Times meanwhile leads on Sunak attacking Truss's tax-cutting plans and saying there was a moral duty to help people struggling with energy bills. He says that scrapping his NI increase would be worth £1,700 to someone on Truss's income, 'a quid a week' to someone on the national living wage and 'precisely zero' to a pensioner.

Neither of these is a sufficiently compelling story for the Mail, which prefers Truss saying that the Navy would continue to patrol the Channel for migrants in small boats, which leads page 10.

Daily Mail, Wednesday, August 17, 2022

Truss tax plan will kick millions into destitution, claims Sunak

By Harriet Line
Chief Political Correspondent

RISHI Sunak last night claimed millions of people risk being 'kicked into destitution' under Liz Truss as he delivered an excoriating attack of her economic policy.

In a brutal blue-on-blue blow, the ex-chancellor said his Tory leadership rival's plans to cut tax to help families through the cost of living crisis would be worth 'precisely zero' to pensioners.

And he told Conservative Party hustings in Perth, Scotland, that her plans would be worth just 'a quid a week' to someone the national living wage.

A Truss campaign source responded: 'It's clear that [Nicola] Sturgeon isn't the only attention seeker in Scotland. It's a shame that Sunak has had to stoop this low just to get a headline.'

Miss Truss has pledged to reverse the national insurance hike to help struggling families, but has not ruled out offering further support. But Mr Sunak said the right way to help people with higher energy bills is through direct support.

He told the hustings: 'The tax cuts that Liz is proposing are worth about £1,700 to someone on her income. For someone working very hard on the national living wage, it's worth about a quid a week.

'And for a pensioner not working, it's worth precisely zero.

'Now I think if that's the policy that the Government adopted, millions of people are at the risk of being kicked into destitution. Mr Sunak's attack came as Miss Truss defended comments in which she claimed British workers need 'more graft'.

In a recording obtained by The Guardian, she suggested Britons lack the 'skill and application' of foreign arrivals. Her comments were recorded when she was Chief Secretary to the Treasury.

Her campaign said Britain needs to 'boost productivity, which leads to higher wages and a better quality of life'.

Cost of living squeeze – Pages 12-13

Now 11 Tory whips say they back Liz

ELEVEN Tory whips came out to back Liz Truss yesterday in a major boost for her campaign.

After chief whip Chris Heaton-Harris removed the requirement for whips to remain neutral in public, MPs including Stuart Anderson and David TC Davies announced their support. Whip James Duddridge said: 'I have known Liz for over 25 years, and I have seen her deliver time and time again.' Rishi Sunak has the backing of five ex-chief whips including Sir Gavin Williamson and Mark Harper.

Navy will still do Channel migrant patrols, vows Liz

By David Barrett
and Michael Blackley

LIZ Truss said yesterday that the Royal Navy will 'absolutely' continue to patrol the Channel if she becomes prime minister.

The Tory leadership frontrunner said that tackling the migrant crisis is an 'absolute priority' and she is prepared to use 'every tool' to crack down on people traffickers illegally bringing people to the UK in small boats.

Her rival Rishi Sunak did not make the same commitment but stressed that the Ministry of Defence has an 'essential' role in the operation.

More than 20,000 migrants have crossed from northern France since the start of the year. The figure is running at 75 per cent higher than at the same point last year.

The leadership candidates' comments come after reports that the Navy is due to pull out of its role in the Channel at the end of January.

Government sources had said the Navy would hand back control to the UK Border Force on January 31 'unless there are ministerial actions', according to The Daily Telegraph.

The MoD was handed £50million by the Government in April to take charge of the Channel crisis under a plan named Operation Isotrope. But the interventions by both candidates make it more likely the MoD will be instructed to carry on its work.

During a visit to a distillery in Elgin, north-east Scotland, Miss Truss said: 'It is an absolute priority to make sure we deal with the issue of small boats and the appalling trade by people traffickers and I will use every tool at my disposal if I'm selected as prime minister to make that happen.'

Asked if that would mean the Navy would continue to perform that role, she said: 'Absolutely.' A Sunak campaign source said: 'Under Rishi's plan, military expertise will be essential in securing control of our borders. He will introduce a taskforce to coordinate the response to every step of an illegal migrant's journey, which will inform the January 2023 review of Operation Isotrope.'

'An absolute priority'

Officials believe any reluctance from within the MoD to carry on with the operation would send the wrong message to people-trafficking gangs, it is understood. The plan's main aim has been to prevent any small boats reaching UK shores unescorted, so they can be processed by officials. But the operation has been criticised by some MPs for being a 'taxi service' for migrants trying to enter Britain.

The Navy has been operating a 260ft offshore patrol vessel to co-ordinate Border Force interceptions, and is shadowing migrant boats with six fast training boats and three rigid-hulled inflatables.

Air support has also been provided by a Wildcat helicopter and Watchkeeper drones fitted with a range of hi-tech sensors which operate out of Lydd airport in Kent.

An MoD spokesman said: 'We are working across government to ensure the conditions are set for defence to hand the task back to the Home Office following the review [next January]. This includes supporting training and capability development.'

■ Campaigners fighting the Government's Rwanda asylum policy yesterday began a legal challenge against a bid to keep parts of an official report on the country under wraps.

Government memos, disclosed last month, revealed the Foreign Office repeatedly warned Downing Street against signing a deal to send migrants to the east African nation to seek asylum because of its poor human rights record. Judgment in the High Court case is expected today.

Comment – Page 16

Naval support: HMS Mersey begins a Channel patrol
Right: Liz Truss visits a Scottish distillery yesterday

The Sunak claim at a hustings in Perth that her tax plans would 'kick millions into destitution' is a shallow hamper. The fourth paragraph is a quote from 'a Truss campaign source' saying: 'It's clear that Sturgeon isn't the only attention seeker in Scotland. It's a shame that Sunak has had to stoop this low just to get a headline.'

The 'more graft' leak makes the penultimate paragraph.

18 August

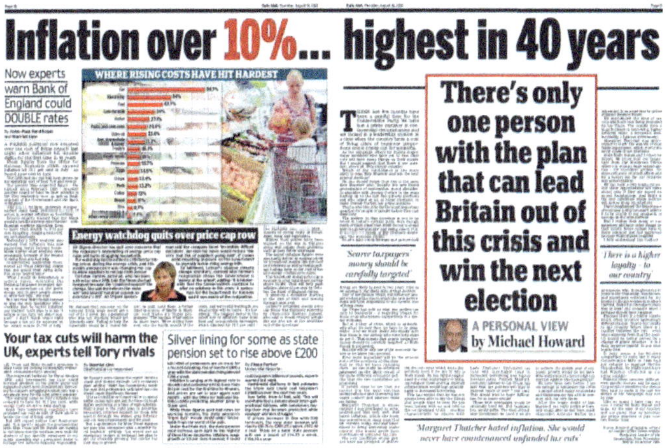
Inflation over 10%... highest in 40 years

Now experts warn Bank of England could DOUBLE rates

WHERE RISING COSTS HAVE HIT HARDEST

Energy watchdog quits over price cap row

Your tax cuts will harm the UK, experts tell Tory rivals

Silver lining for some as state pension set to rise above £200

There's only one person with the plan that can lead Britain out of this crisis and win the next election

A PERSONAL VIEW by Michael Howard

'Scarce taxpayers' money should be carefully targeted'

'There is a higher loyalty – to our country'

'Margaret Thatcher hated inflation. She would never have countenanced unfunded tax cuts'

Inflation hits 10%, the highest for 40 years. This is so alarming that the 10% is printed in red at the top of the 10-11 spread. At the foot of page 10, the Institute for Fiscal Studies says that tax-cutting plans are implausible and would harm the country, while the right-hander has a guest column that is a collector's item. In it Michael Howard says there's only one person with a plan that can lead Britain out of the crisis and win the next election: Rishi Sunak.

Over the page, Truss promises not to back down in the dispute with the EU over the Northern Ireland protocol.

Oh, and Capt Crasheroonie (with an ie) Snoozefest is back in the basement, losing 91,000 party members in a year. Under his leadership, the paper reports, Labour membership dropped from 523,000 at the end of 2020 to 432,000 at the end of 2021 – a 14% decline.

The story does not compare this with other parties. The Conservatives, for example, who have fewer than half as many members. In March 2021, there were 200,000; by the time they voted for their new leader that had fallen by 17.4% to 172,000. But, hey, Johnson was a winner.

Week 7

OBR? WHO EVEN CARES?

19 August

Page 8 — Daily Mail, Friday, August 19, 2022

Most party members didn't want Boris out

Ousted: Boris Johnson

By Whitehall Correspondent

CONSERVATIVE members have condemned MPs for effectively forcing Boris Johnson from office, as tensions continue to mount between the party and its grassroots voters.

According to a YouGov poll, 55 per cent of members believe it was wrong to oust the PM in July amid a dramatic spate of resignations.

Nearly half of them say they would vote for Mr Johnson if he was included on the leadership election ballot and many believe he would make a better leader than either Liz Truss or Rishi Sunak.

The majority of respondants to the survey, which was carried out for Sky News, believe Mr Johnson would beat Sir Keir Starmer at a general election.

Last night, Tory donor and billionaire financier Lord Cruddas accused his party of ignoring members and said it was a 'disgrace' Mr Johnson was not on the ballot.

The peer, who orchestrated a 'Boris ballot' campaign which saw thousands call for the Prime Minister to be included, told the Daily Mail: 'What this poll shows is that Conservative Party members want to keep Boris as their leader.

'So why doesn't the Conservative Party give their members a say over who they want as leader?' He added: 'Whoever wins between Truss and Sunak will never be able to say that they were the members' choice because Boris was never on the ballot and the members have not been asked. It's a disgrace.'

It comes after the Mayor of Tees Valley, Ben Houchen, warned that Red Wall voters would punish the Conservatives at the next election for sidelining Mr Johnson.

In Liz we Truss! Now two-thirds of Tories back her for next PM

By Georgia Edkins
Whitehall Correspondent

LIZ Truss was served a significant boost yesterday as yet another poll put her comfortably on course to become prime minister.

A YouGov survey of Conservative party members revealed 66 per cent were backing Miss Truss compared with 34 per cent supporting Mr Sunak, excluding undecided and non-voters.

Although the 32-point advantage is slightly smaller than in previous polling a fortnight ago, the study of 1,089 people for Sky News between Friday and Wednesday has cemented the Foreign Secretary's position as the frontrunner. Just 13 per cent of those eligible to vote remain undecided and nearly six in ten have already voted.

Last night leading pollster Sir John Curtice said Miss Truss would now almost certainly become prime minister. The professor of politics at Strathclyde University said there was only a tiny chance of victory for Mr Sunak, adding he would be 'extraordinarily surprised' if the Foreign Secretary did not win the leadership.

Of the YouGov survey, he said the pollsters had a 'pretty good record', adding: 'Unless there is something that's gone seriously astray this time it is difficult to believe that Sunak is going to make it.' He told The Times: 'There's a 5 per cent chance that

'Proven her resolve and bravery'

Sunak could win it. Something would have to happen. Truss would have to foul up in some spectacular fashion. Even then it might be too late.'

Sir John said that Miss Truss had come across as the better politician during the race and had stuck to a very clear narrative.

It was confirmed last night that Miss Truss will now take part in a one-to-one interview with the BBC's Nick Robinson, to be shown on August 30.

Miss Truss now has the declared support of more Tory MPs than Mr Sunak, 132 to 124. Allies close to Miss Truss said the figures will be a fresh hammer-blow to the former chancellor, who has until now managed to maintain the support of the majority of Tory parliamentarians.

Yesterday she received a high-profile endorsement from the widow of former Northern Ireland First Minister David Trimble. Writing in The Daily Telegraph, Lady Trimble said that she was 'confident' that her husband's legacy of peace in Northern Ireland would be safe in Miss Truss's hands.

Lord Trimble, who died last month, helped negotiate the 1998 Good Friday Agreement and was awarded a Nobel Peace Prize. Having served as leader of the Ulster Unionist party for a decade from 1995, he joined the Conservatives in 2007.

Lady Trimble wrote: 'I believe that in this contest, Liz Truss has the best record and a viable plan to protect our Union and Northern Ireland's integral place within it. I know David thought the same.

'She has already proven her resolve and bravery in the face of opposition to our most valuable asset, and I am confident that my husband's legacy, peace in Northern Ireland, will be safe with her.'

Mr Sunak faced another bump in the road yesterday when Jacob Rees-Mogg accused him of frustrating attempts to save money in Whitehall while he was chancellor.

Some senior Conservatives have even speculated Mr Sunak could be entering his final days in UK politics. They fear that owing to the personal nature of his campaign there is no chance of him serving in a Truss government.

One said: 'I think he is finished from that perspective. I can see Cabinet positions being given to Suella (Braverman) and Kemi (Badenoch), but not Rishi. I think he's gone and burned his boats.'

With 15 days until the new leader is announced on September 5, Education Secretary James Cleverly said future leadership elections could be wrapped up more quickly.

He told LBC Radio it would be 'legitimate' to review the process.

Today Miss Truss will use hustings in Manchester to pledge to continue levelling up and encouraging investment in the area. Tory MP Jake Berry, chairman of the Northern Research Group, said: 'Liz's ambitious, growth-led vision for the North will deliver on levelling up.

'Stronger regions, empowered to seek investment, centres of educational excellence and a commitment to more money remaining in people's pockets will tackle regional inequality in a Conservative way.'

Any fries with your latest gaffe, Rishi?

Nailed it.

Everyman? Mr Sunak's photo of him in McDonald's

By Harriet Line
Chief Political Correspondent

RISHI Sunak came under fire again yesterday after it emerged his 'go-to' McDonald's order was taken off the menu more than two years' ago.

The Tory leadership hopeful was accused of failing to be 'straight' about his fast food order despite basing his campaign on telling people difficult truths.

In an interview on ITV's This Morning, the ex-chancellor said he likes to order a breakfast wrap from McDonald's if he is dining out with his daughters.

But fans of the restaurant chain were quick to point out it stopped serving the item at the start of the pandemic. In January the company said that breakfast wraps – along with bagels – would not be returning to the menu.

A Whitehall source told the Daily Mail: 'For a man who claims his campaign is based on telling people difficult truths, it's a shame he can't even be straight about his McDonald's order.'

But Mr Sunak's campaign defended the gaffe, saying: 'Rishi has barely seen his kids in the last two and half years since he became chancellor so there has been almost no opportunity to share a McDonald's with them. He's hoping they might consider bringing the breakfast wrap back on the menu.'

The latest blunder comes just months after he was mocked for struggling to use his contactless card at a petrol station. Earlier this week he poked fun at the mistake, posting a photograph of himself paying at a McDonald's self-service machine with the caption: 'Nailed it.'

Asked by presenters what he had ordered, the father of two replied: 'I get a bacon roll with ketchup and the pancakes. But if I'm with my daughters then we get the wrap. If I'm with [my eldest daughter] we get the wrap with the hash brown.'

Mr Sunak has been trailing behind leadership rival Liz Truss in the polls, yet insisted yesterday that he still has a 'shot' at being the next prime minister.

CHILDREN could get dental check-ups at primary schools under Rishi Sunak's plans to improve the nation's teeth.

The Tory leadership hopeful has pledged to launch a pilot scheme so under-11s can see a dentist in the classroom.

The ex-chancellor's vow is part of a five-point plan he says he would enact 'on day one' as PM to 'restore NHS dentistry'.

His proposals include ring-fencing dentistry funding, changing contracts to keep NHS dentists in the health service and 'upskilling' dental teams. He has also pledged to improve education for children and their parents about oral hygiene.

Two-thirds of Conservative members are now backing Truss for PM, although her lead over Sunak has shrunk, according to a new opinion poll. But many are still angry that Johnson was ousted and Lord Cruddas says whoever wins will never be able to claim to be the members' choice because Boris wasn't on the ballot paper.

In the middle of all this, Rishi's contribution is another gaffe – a failure to keep up with menu changes at McDonald's. Asked about his McFavourite, he cited a wrap that hadn't been available for two years. Just shows how out of touch he is. Even with lockdown, no one in the real world goes that long without visiting McDonald's. Paul Dacre doubtless pops in every morning for his breakfast McMuffin.

The story is illustrated by a picture of Sunak paying for a McDonald's order with a contactless card – a picture he posted himself on Instagram with the caption 'nailed it'.

This is a reference to the muddle he got into trying to pay for the petrol he pumped into someone else's car in that embarrassing budget photo-opportunity.

Sunak: I'll put the brakes on smart m-ways

'It goes against common sense'

Javid backs Liz's tax cut plan despite 'black hole' warning

20 August

Another rare top-of-the-page day for Sunak, promising to 'put the brakes' on smart motorways – a cause close to the Mail's heart. Further down, Sajid Javid is backing Truss's tax-cutting plans, in spite of the Office for Budget Responsibility warning that rising borrowing costs would halve the headroom for her proposed measures. In a Times interview, Javid says 'You need to cut taxes to kickstart growth'. A Sunak ally says Truss would have a bigger black hole in the economy than Jeremy Corbyn would have done.

22 August

I will help hardest hit, pledges Truss

Front runner hints at support for families and small businesses

Liz 'is the best bet to preserve the Union'

WHY SHE'S THE ONE WE TRUST

How elderly and vulnerable face plunging into fuel poverty

Millions may get rebates to turn off the dishwasher

With the outcome of the contest pretty much done and dusted, the leadership race makes far fewer appearances these days. But Truss gets a spread when she insists that she will help families and small businesses hardest hit by the rising cost of living.

And three Tory MPs collaborate on a piece saying they like her.

23 August

Sunak is the villain again. This time because he hinted that he would 'snub' any job offer from Truss (none would be forthcoming) and for a 'desperate' attack on her economic plans. He is also accused of failing to hold weekly meetings with the Bank of England governor.

At the foot of the page, John Redwood accuses the OBR of being 'hostile' to Truss's tax plans. In the same story, Truss allies 'indicated that she would not ask the OBR for a forecast ahead of her planned emergency budget next month'.

Sunak-supporting former Treasury minister Mel Stride says that meant she and her chancellor would be 'flying blind', but nobody else seems particularly troubled.

It's not as if choosing not to consult the OBR would cause any problems down the line, is it?

24 August

Allies of Liz Truss are reported to be examining 'radical industry plans for a two-year energy price freeze'. Kwasi Kwarteng – 'strongly tipped to be chancellor if Truss wins next month' – is holding talks on a £100bn scheme to guarantee loans to suppliers so that they can cut prices to consumers.

25 August

Sunak has spent the entire leadership campaign telling Truss that her tax-cutting plans are fairyland economics and would lead to inflation. Now he has ducked questions about whether he would vote for them if she won and tried to put them into practice. This makes the page 8 lead, in which he is accused of 'stunning Tory grandees' with his 'petulant' attacks and a 'scorched earth' policy that would hand the next election to Labour.

Rishi's 'petulant' attacks on Truss will tear Tories apart, say critics

By Jason Groves
Political Editor

RISHI Sunak was last night warned that his 'petulant' attacks on Liz Truss's tax-cutting plans risk handing the next election to Labour.

Bitter pill? Rishi Sunak visits his mother's old pharmacy, where he once worked, in Southampton yesterday

Sunak's Covid regrets

Backing for Liz's £13bn care vow

'Tory grandees' are presumably a layer above 'senior Tories', perhaps a little more experienced. But none is identified and no one in the story seems stunned. The people accusing Sunak of petulance etc are anonymous Truss 'allies', while the only other figure named is former minister David Jones, saying Sunak must accept the result of the contest and that the whole party must unite behind the winner.

The leader – in a newspaper where anyone in any other walk of life (or in any other political party) who deviates from a previously stated position is pilloried for hypocrisy – makes clear that a Tory MP's duty is to back their prime minister and to follow them into the division lobby, no matter how loudly and repeatedly they may have argued against a policy in the past.

Under the headline 'Don't waste energy on petulance, Mr Sunak', it says:

> *It reflects incredibly badly on Rishi Sunak that he refuses to say whether he'd vote for Liz Truss's emergency budget if, as expected, she wins the leadership contest.*
>
> *If he and his supporters don't stop the 'blue-on-blue' attacks, they may as well throw open No 10's doors to Labour, which could destroy the Conservative Party.*
>
> *Mr Sunak must put party and country first, not petulant personal grievances.*

In editorial after editorial, the Mail urges Tory MPs to put their 'party and country first' – with party always taking precedence over country. That is presumably because the paper sincerely believes that the wellbeing of the country depends on having a Conservative government, which in turn requires a united and disciplined party. Loyalty to the leader is non-negotiable. But this applies only to Conservatives. Keir Starmer is consistently under fire for having 'campaigned to get Jeremy Corbyn into No 10'. Which is kind of what you'd have expected him – or any Labour MP – to have done when Corbyn was their leader.

Week 8

BRING ON TRUSSONOMICS

26 August

With hike in gas and electricity cap coming today, a cheering pledge in article for Mail...

TRUSS: I'LL GET YOU THROUGH THE ENERGY BILL CRISIS

LIZ Truss today pledges 'immediate support' to help with soaring power bills if she becomes prime minister.

The price cap is expected to be raised to more than £3,500 per household today – almost treble the figure a year ago.

Analysts say bills could rise by a further £1,000 in January, with more pain in April as Vladimir Putin 'weaponises' his gas resources.

By **Jason Groves** Political Editor

But writing in the Daily Mail, Miss Truss says she would use an emergency budget next month to 'ensure support is on its way to get through these tough times'.

Energy firms warn that millions of families may be unable to pay their bills this winter without government help. And business leaders predict that many firms will go under unless action is taken to rein in their exorbitant power costs.

Miss Truss and her rival for No 10, Rishi Sunak, have both pledged to continue a £15billion support package unveiled in June.

But the Foreign Secretary today indicates she will go significantly further to ease the squeeze on cash-strapped homes. She says Britain is

Turn to Page 6

The new energy price cap is to be announced today, and is expected to mean average bills of around £3,500. So Truss writes another guest column to make the first leadership campaign splash for two-and-a-half weeks. Her 'cheering pledge' to help families includes lifting the fracking moratorium and inspires more speculation on Kwarteng's £100bn plan to freeze bills for two years, even though insiders 'played down the prospect of it being approved'.

Rishi Sunak is still warning against 'unfunded tax cuts', but is reported to have done a U-turn and said that he would vote for any measures Truss put forward. He hadn't actually said he would not vote for her package – he had declined to say one way or the other – so it's a bit of a stretch to call it a U-turn.

COST OF LIVING CRUNCH

By Liz Truss

I know how hard it is for millions of you, but I'll ensure support is on its way

Truss pledges to end ban on fracking in UK energy boost

Q&A

by Sean Poulter

Labour plan to freeze bills 'has £8billion black hole'

Thousands could 'disconnect' from their gas and electricity

Anyway, the leader again endorses Truss's strategy, says she must stick to her guns and comes up with a novel suggestion:

> *She must face down the irreconcilable eco-lobby and the obstructionists. Why not, though, win round communities living in the shadow of fracking operations or nuclear plants by offering them free energy?*
>
> *For 30 years, successive governments have stuck their fingers in their ears and hoped the problem of Britain's energy needs simply disappeared.*
>
> *Our woes show just how important it is that a Tory PM finally grasps the nettle.*

27 August

Energy prices dominate the news and make the lead and two spreads for the Mail. The two candidates for PM do not appear to have anything to say about this, but Jason Groves has a warning for Liz Truss and her stated dislike for handouts at the foot of one of the spreads. She must, he writes, balance her Tory instincts with reality.

Andrew Neil is back in the Saturday essay slot with more warnings. Having cautioned Truss earlier this month that her biggest enemy would be not Starmer's Labour but 'the Left Blob', Neil now tells her to watch out for her parliamentary colleagues (who are again drinking in their favourite bar).

Careerists, One Nation Tories, hardline Brexiteers and backbenches full of 'grandees', such as Gove, Sunak and Raab, will all be on her case. Keeping discipline will be difficult. Neil's advice is to avoid gimmicks, to quietly ditch most of her campaign trail promises and to target help where it's needed.

> *It's a tall order, even for a prime minister of great experience and proven competence. Truss has neither attribute. But her own troops need to give her a chance. If they cut up rough from the start, they have no chance of succeeding.*
>
> *The Tories are in the last-chance saloon. If they make a hash of this winter then the game is up. They won't have time to recover before an election.*

Neil doesn't seem convinced Truss is up to the job. Maybe he didn't get the memo. For on the same page, the leader 'fervently hopes' that she is on her way to Downing Street. Once again it instructs Tory MPs to show unity and competence because 'history teaches us that voters ditch parties at war with themselves'.

> *In ten days' time, Britain will have a new prime minister. To a public sick of the vain posturing of the political class, that moment can't come too soon.*
>
> *For it will mark the end of what has been a tortuous and needlessly vituperative Tory leadership contest, which feels like it has dragged on since Methuselah was a boy.*
>
> *True, Liz Truss and Rishi Sunak have used the campaign to spell out their respective visions of how to revitalise the country. But it has seemed like the rival camps have spent more time throwing rocks at each other than explaining exactly how they'd solve the manifold problems coming down the track.*
>
> *Not only is this a gift for Sir Keir Starmer, the BBC and the Tory party's foes, who will wheel out the bad-tempered soundbites right up until the next election. The internecine warfare has also given the dangerous impression that there is a vacuum of political leadership at the heart of government.*
>
> *Streets ahead in the polls, Miss Truss seems destined for No 10. The Mail fervently hopes so. We believe the Foreign Secretary to be an authentic standard-bearer for low-tax, pro-growth, small-state Conservatism - and she has the imagination, boldness and fortitude to succeed in the top job.*

Quite a few hits on the leader bingo card there – low-tax, pro-growth, small-state plus internecine warfare, which has made a good half-dozen appearances through the campaign.

29 August

Page 6 — Daily Mail, Monday, August 29, 2022

Truss's tax bid to help families with cost crunch

By Jason Groves
Political Editor

LIZ Truss is poised to raise income tax thresholds as part of a major package of measures designed to ease the cost of living crunch.

The Foreign Secretary will also consider the 'nuclear option' of temporarily cutting the headline rate of VAT by 5 per cent, at an estimated cost of £30billion.

But sources said the leadership frontrunner has all but ruled out adding to the universal £400 energy bill discount agreed by her rival Rishi Sunak earlier this year.

Instead, direct support is likely to focus on targeted measures, such as increasing the winter fuel allowance for pensioners and helping those on universal credit.

Miss Truss had already pledged to hold an emergency budget next month to reverse some of the tax rises imposed by Mr Sunak, including those to national insurance and corporation tax.

She has also promised to suspend green levies on energy bills. But, as the scale of the crisis becomes clearer, she is now considering emergency tax cuts to put more cash back in people's pockets.

A senior ally of Miss Truss said she was 'certain' to end the four-year freeze in income tax thresholds which was brought in by Mr Sunak last year to help pay off the huge cost of dealing with Covid.

'Recession is not inevitable'

The freeze, which was forecast to raise £8.1billion a year, was introduced at a time when inflation was below two per cent.

But with inflation now standing at 9.4 per cent and forecast by some to double next year, the freeze is set to raise vast sums and drag millions of people into paying more tax.

A senior ally of Miss Truss said: 'One thing you can be certain of is the freeze on thresholds is going to end early.

'When inflation is running at 10 per cent you cannot have the thresholds frozen because you will have people paying a higher proportion of tax on their income at a time when bills are going through the roof.'

Tax cuts are being considered to stave off a recession, which Miss Truss insisted yesterday was 'not inevitable'. She told the Mail on Sunday she had a 'clear plan to get Britain through this storm and out the other side'.

She added: 'A recession is not inevitable, but we need to make sure we don't talk ourselves into one. I don't believe in managed decline. And I won't accept it. I believe in hope over fear.'

Business Secretary Kwasi Kwarteng, who has been tipped to serve as Miss Truss's chancellor, is expected to look at raising the basic rate threshold of £12,570 and the 40 per cent higher rate threshold of £50,270.

He will also consider bringing forward a planned 1p cut in the basic rate of income tax, which is not due to come in until 2024.

The Treasury has drawn up proposals for a temporary cut in the headline rate of VAT by either 2.5 per cent or 5 per cent from its current rate of 20 per cent. A campaign source declined to comment in detail but said 'nothing is off the table in terms of support'.

However, another source said Miss Truss had 'ruled out' further universal discounts to energy bills.

Boris Johnson considered cutting the headline rate of VAT earlier this year, but the measure was blocked by Mr Sunak.

Economist Patrick Minford, whose work has been cited by Miss Truss, yesterday backed a VAT cut to head off a recession.

He told Times Radio: 'This crisis is triggering households to cut consumption and causing recession. It is important for fiscal policy to move against that, which is why it makes sense to cut VAT or income tax. But VAT can be done more quickly.'

However, another ally of Miss Truss said that the measure was 'badly targeted', adding: 'The big problem people have is with energy bills and food costs.

'Energy only has a 5 per cent VAT rate and food doesn't attract VAT at all.'

Allies of Mr Sunak yesterday warned that a cut to VAT would be 'incredibly regressive', helping the better off far more than the poor. Former Cabinet minister Simon Hart, who is backing Mr Sunak, warned that the crisis needed concerted action to tackle inflation rather than short-term tax cuts.

He said: 'This is not going to be easy. This is not going to be resolved by just an eye-catching tax cut on day one.'

Comment – Page 14

Solutions Liz could turn to as Prime Minister

By Political Editor

CUTTING VAT

Proposal: The Treasury has drawn up options for a temporary cut in VAT of 2.5 or 5 per cent.

Pros: The move would cut inflation in the short term and deliver an immediate boost to both household incomes and the economy, helping to stave off a recession.

Cons: Expensive, at a cost of up to £30billion. Critics point out that energy and food bills attract little or no VAT bill.

Plans: Liz Truss last week

RAISING INCOME TAX THRESHOLDS

Proposal: Plans to raise both the tax-free personal allowance and the threshold at which people start paying 40 per cent tax.

Pros: Would bring an early end to Rishi Sunak's four-year freeze on thresholds, would prevent millions of people being forced to pay a high proportion of their income in tax. With inflation at almost 10 per cent it is hard to justify continuing the freeze.

Cons: Would deprive the Treasury of a huge windfall which could be used to fund other support measures.

CUTTING THE BASIC RATE OF INCOME TAX

Proposal: Bring forward a 1p cut in the basic rate, which is not due until 2024.

Pros: Would put immediate cash in the pockets of 27million people who pay income tax and is in line with her approach of allowing people to keep more of their cash.

Cons: Mr Sunak has argued cutting income tax now would fuel inflation, leaving everyone worse off in the long-run.

DIRECT HELP WITH BILLS THIS WINTER

Proposal: The Treasury has put forward a range of proposals for helping the worst off this winter.

Pros: Measures such as raising the pensioners' winter fuel allowance and increasing universal credit would directly target those people on 'fixed incomes' who need the most help.

Cons: Does nothing for those on middle incomes. Chancellor Nadhim Zahawi warned this weekend people on £45,000 salaries may need help – well above the level for claiming universal credit.

ENDING VAT ON ENERGY BILLS

Proposal: Allies of Miss Truss are urging her to borrow Mr Sunak's plan to scrap the 5 per cent VAT on energy bills.

Pros: Would use Britain's post-Brexit freedoms to offer everyone savings of around £170 a year.

Cons: Cutting VAT would be difficult in Northern Ireland, where EU rules still apply. The £170 cut is relatively modest when the energy price cap has almost trebled to £3,549.

More speculation on the various measures prime minister Truss might adopt to ease the cost of living crisis. These now include raising income tax thresholds and – again – cutting VAT on fuel (Kwarteng did neither). A panel runs through the options and a basement story says people could be offered a 25% discount on fuel bills if they agree to fracking in their areas.

The leader says it is vital that the new PM hits the ground running and welcomes the moves it believes are under consideration

Of course, she mustn't inadvertently fuel the inflationary spiral. But leaving more money in people's pockets would help them pay for power, while boosting the economy more generally, supporting consumer and business confidence - and possibly staving off a recession.

And the cherry on the top? It's a solution rooted in Tory ideology.

Week 9

FIZZY LIZZIE CROWNED

3 September

As top QC delivers devastating verdict on 'fundamentally flawed' Boris inquiry, MPs and peers rally round to demand...

NOW END THE PARTY PROBE WITCH-HUNT

MPs faced mounting pressure last night to halt the Partygate probe into Boris Johnson after a top QC called it 'unfair' and 'fundamentally flawed'.

In a bombshell legal analysis, Lord Pannick said the parliamentary inquiry would be declared unlawful were it not protected from challenge in the courts.

He claimed the approach of the Commons privileges committee was 'wrong in principle' and pointed out that it

By **Martin Beckford** Policy Editor

featured 'political opponents' of Mr Johnson who have 'made personal criticisms of his conduct'.

The barrister also warned the inquiry risked having a wider 'chilling effect' on ministers if they could be punished for inadvertently making a mistake when addressing the Commons.

The committee is investigating whether the Prime Minister misled Parliament with his statements on lockdown gatherings.

But it has been accused of moving the goalposts after deciding it would not take his intentions into account when he told MPs last year that 'the rules were followed at all times'.

Yesterday's explosive verdict by Lord Pannick, who has acted against the Government in high-profile Supreme Court cases, was a major boost for Mr Johnson and his supporters.

The advice prompted fresh calls for the inquiry's terms to be changed or for the entire case to be dropped.

Mr Johnson is preparing to leave Downing Street next week after either Liz Truss or Rishi Sunak is named as the new Tory leader. He and the winner will fly to Balmoral in Scotland for the official handover of power with

Turn to Page 6

After a quiet few days when the Mail appeared to lose its appetite for the Tory contest – Nadine Dorries might stay as culture secretary, Truss might dump green levies for energy firms, the new PM will have to go to Balmoral to kiss hands because the Queen is too frail to travel to London – the final vote-counting weekend is marked by a news spread on the expectation that Truss will swiftly lift the ban on fracking, plus her latest vowing – this time to make the country succeed.

PM Liz 'to ditch ban on fracking in days'

No10 favourite wants to boost UK energy supplies

How did eco-warriors get into Parliament?

LET THE PEOPLE DECIDE

CITIZENS ASSEMBLY NOW

I will do all I can to make UK succeed, vows Truss

Schools 'may cut staff to pay bills'

Miss Underestimated

The paper is far more interested in the Partygate 'witch-hunt' and devotes the splash and two spreads to its fallen hero. The first rejoices in Lord Pannick's view that the investigation was fundamentally flawed, unfair and a threat to democracy that could put every future prime minister at risk. This opinion has added cachet because Pannick has previously challenged the government in court, which proves he's no establishment patsy.

'Every future PM could be at risk'

10 KEY POINTS that left an eminent QC fearing for democracy

Stephen Glover

Now it's quite clear: Natural justice has been denied in the cause of ruining Boris Johnson

Labour MP hits out at 'bizarre' legal opinion

The second is Sarah Vine's up close and personal take on Boris, a man too nice to be PM.

SARAH VINE has been alongside the PM — who leaves office on Tuesday — during some of the most pivotal moments of his life. His enemies will sneer at her verdict — but they don't know him like she does...

by Sarah Vine

Boris's real tragedy is that he was too nice to rule over the Nasty Party

Boris was a loose cannon, led by instinct

Relatable and likeable, he was also vulnerable

Tory MPs smelt blood and began to circle

Way back in the paper, though, is a three-page essay on Truss's rise to the brink of power, characterising her as 'Miss Underestimated'.

She's set to become our third female Prime Minister next week. Critics say she's just a political chameleon. But the Mail's spoken to her teachers, relatives and old friends to discover what makes Liz Truss tick. And one thing is clear: she's always been...

MISS UNDERESTIMATED

by Richard Kay and Andrew Pierce

'My dad would say she cheated to win [at board games]. She was someone who HAD to win

TRUSS'S YOUNGEST BROTHER, FRANCIS

Brought up in a LibDem-voting, Guardian-reading activist household, where a weekend not spent marching for CND or supporting the Greenham Common women was a weekend wasted, Truss had decided at ten that she wanted to be a politician and in her teens that she wanted to be PM. It was 'hardly surprising that her exposure to agit-prop dogma drew her first to the sandal-wearing, placard-bearing Liberal Democrats, the perennial party of protest'.

But now she had 'barely concealed contempt for liberal group-think' – a recasting of her political outlook that, the essayists report, triggered family friction, soul-searching and anguish.

Truss and her team were now spending the weekend hunkered down at Chevening, putting the finishing touches to a Cabinet line-up that she hoped would 'not just end the government paralysis which has existed since Boris Johnson was forced from office, but also transform the fortunes of a country facing the greatest cost of living crisis in 50 years'.

She may have the monotone of the speaking clock, but she was now a resounding Tory favourite, and internal party enemies and the Labour Opposition needed to learn quickly that Truss would be no pushover.

The childhood aspiration was matched by a steely ambition not merely to become prime minister, but to 'do something' with the position. A 'friend' explains: 'She will want to leave the country in a better place than it is when she comes in.'

5 September

Daily Mail

MONDAY, SEPTEMBER 5, 2022

Daily newspaper of the year 90p 55p to subscribers*

VAR SUCKING JOY OUT OF FOOTBALL
THE VERDICT
PULLOUT INSIDE

Subscribe today and get your Daily Mail... FOR ONLY 55p ...the same price as 10 years ago
SUBSCRIBE AT: mailsubs.co.uk/rollback
See Page 4 - Terms apply

After Have I Got News For You c-word jibe at PM, corporation's new flagship politics show sparks fresh anti-Tory bias storm

NOW BBC COMIC MOCKS LIZ TRUSS

It's results day and the Mail is cross with the BBC for having Joe Lycett on Laura Kuenssberg's inaugural Sunday politics show. So cross that it devotes the splash and two inside pages to proclaiming 'it's no time for this sort of nonsense', before reporting the PM-in-waiting's promise that she won't let people 'talk this great country down'.

(Yesterday's Mail on Sunday was cross with the BBC because Have I Got News for You host Jack Dee quoted a Tory MP calling Johnson the C-word. It wasn't, however, cross with either The Times or the MP who threw the insult.)

The leader column is thankful that the contest is finally over and that Truss – who has been like a 'caged animal' for the past few days – is ready to hit the ground running with a detailed plan to deal with soaring energy bills within a week, and an emergency tax-cutting budget within a month. Let the fightback begin!

Though the poorest will require most support, she stressed that tax cuts should not be seen just 'through the prism of redistribution'. They are for the benefit of all and intended to stimulate growth. And with growth comes prosperity. As John F Kennedy famously put it, a rising tide lifts all boats.

This was once a fundamental principle of Conservatism but it has been obscured by the Covid emergency, during which massive state handouts became the norm. This has led to borrowing at levels never before seen in peacetime and took the national debt to nearly £2.4trillion - money that will have to be repaid by future generations.

Miss Truss is right to stress that it is only through growth and improved productivity that this mountain of debt will be reduced and the public finances put back on track.

We cannot and should not expect state handouts to cover every misfortune...

But we are not, as the professional catastrophists love to present it, approaching some kind of Armageddon. There is nothing we haven't faced and come through in the past.

Miss Truss promised to be honest with the country about the scale of the problems ahead. But, like Boris Johnson, she has faith that, together, we will overcome them...

Through her vision, energy and initiative, the Tory fightback can begin today.

6 September

HARRY & MEGHAN BOOED IN MANCHESTER SEE PAGES 4-5

Daily Mail

TUESDAY, SEPTEMBER 6, 2022 Daily newspaper of the year 90p 55p to subscribers*

No PM since Maggie has faced a tougher in-tray than Liz Truss. Now she plans a 'shock and awe' strategy on energy bills, tax and the NHS to stamp her mark on Britain

FEMALE PMs: IT'S TORIES...3 LABOUR...0

Cometh the hour, cometh the woman...

LIZ Truss will freeze energy bills, slash taxes and shake up the NHS in a 'shock and awe' bid to stamp her authority on government.

By **Jason Groves** Political Editor

The new Tory leader, who succeeds Boris Johnson as Prime Minister today, will launch a policy blitz aimed at uniting her warring party and decisively dealing with the cost of living crisis.

Her ministers were last night locked in talks with energy bosses to thrash out details of a 'freeze' in bills that could last two years and cost £100billion. Miss Truss was confirmed as leader of the Conservative Party yesterday after defeating Rishi Sunak 57:43 in a vote by members.

In her acceptance speech she vowed to 'deliver, deliver, deliver'. She added: 'I will deliver a bold plan to cut taxes and grow our economy. I will deliver on the energy crisis dealing with people's energy bills, but

Turn to Page 6

The hiatus is finally over and Liz Truss will today become our prime minister. The Mail celebrates with a poster front that says she plans a 'shock and awe' strategy to 'stamp her mark' on Britain.

LIZ'S SHOCK AND AWE

Unite or die – Tories warned

Johnson, May, Cameron and IDS call on the whole party to back leader

CONGRATULATIONS FROM HER HUSBAND

HANDSHAKE SNUB FOR RISHI

HENRY DEEDES SKETCH

Liz let slip a giddy chuckle. Good God... she'd done it!

LITTLEJOHN

Seven inside news pages are supplemented by a full-page leader, Richard Littlejohn saying 'fizzy Lizzie' will need the hide of a rhino, and Andrew Neil urging her to push ahead with fracking.

Neil says that she will have to junk most of the 'ridiculous' 149 policy pledges she made on the campaign trail and that only two tax cuts – the NI and corporation tax reversals – should go ahead.

Combining multibillion handouts to ease the energy pain with multibillion tax cuts would send the pound plummeting and lock in high inflation, he writes

Hold that thought, as they say.

There are signs, he continues, that Team Truss realise they can't have it all:

> *On Sunday, the likely new chancellor, Kwasi Kwarteng, took to the columns of the Financial Times to reassure the markets that, though there would be some 'fiscal loosening' (i.e. more debt), a Truss government would be 'fiscally responsible' (no magic money tree)...*
>
> *For the moment, she must focus on cushioning as many millions of households as possible from the energy crisis. In the first six months of her premiership, nothing else will really matter, even tax cuts, however much Tory tax-cutters complain.*

And once again, Neil recognises a reality that escapes the leader writers:

> *The wellbeing of families up and down the land will depend on her getting this right. So will her future as Prime Minister, which will be short-lived if she gets it wrong.*

The leader, meanwhile, is still in mourning for Johnson – admitting that it is repeating itself by starting 'As the Mail has said many times, this was a contest that should never have happened.'

It then goes on to repeat itself some more, replaying some of the leader writers' greatest hits:

- It's to the eternal shame of many in the party that they conspired with his enemies to bring him down.
- They succumbed to a fit of collective hysteria.
- They were cowed by a 'relentless Twitter tirade from the Left, a hostile broadcast media and embittered Remainers'.
- They betrayed their most potent electoral asset for a 'string of political molehills that were cynically jammed together and fabricated into a mountain of humbug'.
- Historians will be baffled that a birthday cake that never came out of its Tupperware box could be deployed as a lethal weapon.
- Set against his achievements – getting Brexit through, the vaccine miracle, defying Putin over Ukraine – his lapses were trivial.
- It's a tragedy and a travesty.

But back to the present and the 'welcome Truss' editorial, which has another of its greatest hits in the headline: 'Tories drinking in the last-chance saloon'. They must, it says, get behind their new leader and she, in turn, should restore unity by appointing a government of all talents to reverse Labour's ten-point lead in the polls.

The Tory party is in the last-chance saloon. If MPs don't unite behind Liz Truss, oblivion beckons – for them AND Britain

Daily Mail COMMENT

If Miss Truss can't turn that around, oblivion beckons.

Sir Keir Starmer can scarcely hope to win an overall majority, but he could cobble together a coalition of chaos.

With the support of Lib Dems, Scots Nats, Greens and any other fringe party he could drag in, Sir Keir could become a lame-duck PM at the head of a shambolic minority government.

In short order we could see the break-up of the United Kingdom, a tax and spend orgy, the effects of which would dwarf today's economic woes, and proportional representation, consigning the mother of Parliaments to the muddle and misery of endless coalition.

The Mail never contemplates the possibility that the Labour party might be able to secure an overall majority without being bolstered by other 'cranks' or actually run the country. It is a given that a Labour government would wreck the economy, ruin our culture and destroy the union. It does not explain why it thinks the latter or consider that Brexit is more likely to do the job, with the SNP pressing for another independence referendum and anger over the Northern Ireland protocol reviving talk of a united Ireland.

On economic policy, the editorial continues:

> *Miss Truss made clear she would be looking for Conservative solutions to the country's problems. This means reverting to a low-tax, small-state economy...she has pledged to scrap the recent National Insurance hike, green levies and forthcoming Corporation Tax rises.*
>
> *Mr Sunak and the Treasury blob say this policy is 'counter-productive', and will fuel inflation and increase debt. But let's not forget that these are the very people who have allowed UK taxation to rise to a 70-year high.*
>
> *Such fiscal punishment is distinctly un-Conservative and simply cannot go on. By reducing the tax burden, the new Prime Minister hopes to stimulate growth and investment and raise consumer confidence.*
>
> *Many economists also say it won't work. But they said the same about Thatcherism. Their track record of being wrong is almost legendary.*

7 September

HISTORIC SPECIAL EDITION

Daily Mail

WEDNESDAY, SEPTEMBER 7, 2022 Daily newspaper of the year 90p 55p to subscribers*

4.50PM 5.07PM

Downpour St: Crowds huddle in the rain, minutes before Liz Truss strides into No10 in a burst of sunshine

How the Left-wing Twitterati crowed as the heavens opened just before Liz Truss arrived in Downing Street for her big speech. Then, in a moment loaded with cheering symbolism, the skies cleared - and our new PM declared...

TOGETHER WE CAN RIDE OUT THE STORM

JAN MOIR Witnesses history

AS new Prime Minister Liz Truss swept towards No 10 in her motorcade, primed and ready to make the most important speech of her life, the weather took a turn for the worse.

Oh dear, oh no, not now! Inky storm clouds gathered, the heavens duly opened and a late summer rainstorm threatened to wreck her big moment on the pavement outside Downing Street.

The omens of this biblical deluge weren't lost on anyone. There was gloating on social media, much titteration amongst the Twitterati and excited acknowledgement of the looming calamity over on the BBC's live coverage. 'Boris took over on

Turn to Page 4

Formally asked by the Queen to form a government, Truss gets to work with the promise of a two-year energy price freeze and the prediction that 'together we can ride out the storm'.

An 'historic special edition' of the Mail includes a colour splash by Jan Moir angled on the rain giving way to the sun as Truss walked into Downing Street and celebrating her 'lack of polish' as proof of her authenticity.

Inside, some 12 pages on the new administration focus on the prime minister's desire to build an 'aspiration nation', and on her new cabinet, which may be diverse but – contrary to the advice from the Mail and its columnists – excludes anyone who didn't back her leadership or was too slow off the mark in doing so.

WE CAN RIDE OUT THE STORM

My bold plan to build an Aspiration Nation

- Truss vows 'action every day' to get UK working again
- Brutal cull of Team Rishi as she appoints the loyalists
- Energy plan tomorrow will freeze bills at £2,500
- NHS reforms to ensure everyone can get to see GP

Strong as the storm may be, I know the British people are stronger

HER SPEECH IN FULL

Guru gunning for green taxes

City Editor Alex Brummer applauds her 'audacious' energy price plan, saying it will help families and curb inflation. She has, he writes, got off to a flying start, although he notes that it will be a challenge for Kwarteng to finance the £140 billion of borrowing her plans will probably require.

Money Mail in the back of the book takes an equally optimistic view with the question "Will a blast of Trussonomics put cash in YOUR pocket?"

The leader says that if the Tories are to win the next election, Truss hasn't a second to waste in improving people's lives. It also emphasises that the economic crisis is global – which is all the fault of the pandemic and Putin.

8 September

Read this paper on your tablet or phone for... £1 FOR 12 WEEKS www.mailsubs.co.uk SEE PAGES 16-17

Daily Mail

THURSDAY, SEPTEMBER 8, 2022 Daily newspaper of the year 90p 55p to subscribers*

First day at new school for George, Charlotte and Louis

SEE PAGES 4-5

All together: William, Kate and the little Cambridges yesterday

LIZ'S ENERGY REVOLUTION

PM will today freeze bills at £2,500, launch new dash for North Sea gas... and restart fracking

By Jason Groves
Political Editor

LIZ Truss will today freeze fuel bills, end the fracking ban and signal a new era of oil and gas exploration in the North Sea.

Unveiling her energy revolution, the new Prime Minister is set to announce immediate help for struggling families and businesses this winter, while also setting out plans for a major increase in domestic supplies.

Miss Truss will freeze average bills at around £2,500 – lifting the uncertainty hanging over millions of households.

The freeze, which is set to last for at least 18 months, could cost taxpayers anything up to £150billion – more than double the cost of the furlough scheme.

The Prime Minister will also confirm a package of help for businesses facing the threat of closure due to soaring energy costs. Yesterday Miss Truss said the support package is essential if the

Turn to Page 6

It's the first day at school for the Cambridge kids and the first PMQs for Liz Truss, and now we can look forward to the official unveiling of the much-trailed energy package with bills being frozen and a return to fracking. Welcome to the revolution.

There are twelve pages on this, including an inside story that asks: 'Why is climate tsar claiming that lifting ban won't help energy prices?'

It might have asked the same question of new chancellor Kwasi Kwarteng, who had said the same thing when he was business secretary in February – and even written about it for the Mail on Sunday in March. Calling for investment in clean energy, he wrote that it would be madness to turn off North Sea oil and gas lines in the interim. But onshore fracking was 'very different'. 'Those calling for its return misunderstand the situation we find ourselves in. If we lifted the fracking moratorium, it would take up to a decade to extract sufficient volumes – and it would come at a high cost for communities and our precious countryside. 'No amount of shale gas from hundres of wells dotted across rural England would be enough to lower the European price any times soon. And with the best will in the world, private companies are not going to sell the shale gas they produce to UK consumers below the market price. They are not charities, after all.'

There is more on the new cabinet, a column by Stephen Glover describing Truss as more radical than Thatcher at her most radical, and a leader saying she had got off to a 'fine start'.

A page lead in the middle of the coverage notes that the pound dipped to a 37-year low against the dollar.

Weeks 10 and 11

RIP, YOUR MAJESTY

9 September

ENERGY PRICE CAP

Liz: I'll save families over £1,000 a year

- PM unveils package to freeze average bills at £2,500
- £100bn-plus plan includes new dash for gas and oil
- Business to get 'equivalent' help... windfall tax ruled out

HOW MUCH WILL YOU PAY?

'Extraordinary measures'

So how will it work, how much will it cost, who will benefit and for how long?

Fracking ban lifted and gas could flow within six months

Jabs tsar leads new taskforce

'It's time we seized this opportunity'

Costly yes, but move could ward off a recession, say economists

The death of the Queen occupies the first 83 pages of the paper – the second 'historic special edition' in three days – interrupted only by the puzzles. But Truss pops up at the first available opportunity on pages 84-85 to claim that her plans will save families more than £1,000 a year.

10 September

ELIZABETH R 1926-2022

New King's audience with Britain's new PM

His Majesty receives Liz Truss at the palace after PM hails an 'era of hope'

Carrie: She was so warm and kind... we were lucky that she was our Queen

Here is (or are) the news: the new prime minister has her first audience with the new king, having 'hailed a new era of hope and progress'.

The official period of national mourning means that the business of running the country is put on hold for a further ten days. It was also supposed to be ten days free of politics, but it didn't quite work out that way. The planning and leaking continue unabated – and unchallenged, since there is no Parliament in session and no official announcements that can be questioned.

12 September

The royal coverage is scaled back to 29 pages, with Truss again occupying the first 'normal' page. Here she has a 'boost' with nine out of ten voters backing her freeze on fuel bills, according to a poll commissioned by the Mail. What's not to like about not having to spend more to keep warm?

The poll also found that 72 per cent wanted a windfall tax on energy giants (ruled out by Truss), that 55 per cent wanted an immediate general election, that more people thought Starmer would be a better prime minister than Truss, and that Labour had a seven-point lead over the Tories when it came to voting intentions for the next election.

13 September

The King has announced that the national mourning will continue for a week after the state funeral on Monday, but Downing Street says Parliament will return before that and that the 'emergency tax-cutting budget' will go ahead this month.

16 September

The chancellor is reported to be abolishing the cap on bankers' bonuses imposed by the EU after the financial crash of 2008. The Mail is all for it, saying that what looks like bad timing and a PR disaster will make the City more attractive to international talent and ultimately make us all more prosperous.

> *Mr Kwarteng should ignore the Left's outraged howls and dig his heels in on this policy. His job is to make the right calls for the economy - not to wilt before banker-bashing populism.*

17 September

With the date set for next Friday, 'emergency mini-budget' leaks keep coming. This time it's how quickly the national insurance increase will be reversed.

19 September

It's the day of the funeral, but still the leaks flow; Kwarteng – in Tommy Cooper 'Just like that' pose - is preparing to pull a rabbit out of the hat. Now we're looking at an earlier cut in the base rate of income tax and a reversal of the planned increase in corporation tax. Investment zones also rear their head.

Page 40

Will income tax be cut in Kwarteng's budget for growth?

By Harriet Line
Chief Political Correspondent

KWASI Kwarteng could fast-track plans to cut 1p off income tax in a 'bold' and 'growth-focused' mini-budget this week.

The Chancellor is said to be considering bringing forward Rishi Sunak's plans to reduce the basic rate of income tax from 20p to 19p in the pound.

Mr Sunak said in March that this would take effect in 2024, but speculation is mounting that his successor could fast-track the move.

However, the decision could be deferred until the Government holds a formal Budget – possibly in November – which will be accompanied by an Office for Budget Responsibility forecast.

Sources told The Mail on Sunday Mr Kwarteng is planning a top-secret 'knock-out surprise measure' – described as a 'proper rabbit out of the hat moment'. Whitehall insiders said last night that the mini-budget would be 'bold' and 'growth-focused', but declined to confirm the reports.

Friday's emergency mini-budget will be one of the most significant fiscal interventions in the past century.

'Make London more globally competitive'

The Chancellor is expected to confirm plans to reverse the 1.25 percentage point national insurance rise as soon as November and say that next year's planned increase in corporation tax will not go ahead.

Liz Truss is also reportedly considering plans to slash personal taxes and business levies in new 'investment zones'. Those who live and work in the low-tax areas envisaged by the Prime Minister could see their own contributions cut, with the burden also lightened for businesses.

The proposed 'investment zones', dubbed 'full-fat freeports', were a staple of Miss Truss's campaign for the Tory leadership. She said that under her plan these areas would benefit from low tax, reduced planning restrictions and regulations tailored on a case-by-case basis.

The Sun on Sunday reported that the new PM is now weighing up whether personal taxes could be cut for people working there.

Mr Kwarteng will use Friday's statement to push ahead with plans for City deregulation, having told bank chiefs he wants a 'Big Bang 2.0' – in reference to Margaret Thatcher's sudden deregulation of financial markets – to make London the capital of global finance again.

Last week, Treasury sources also confirmed that he was considering scrapping the cap on bankers' bonuses to make the City of London more globally competitive.

Ministers are also said to have discussed whether environmental protections could be watered down in these 'investment zones' to clear the way for new developments.

The Government is reportedly looking at the West Midlands, Thames Estuary, Tees Valley, West Yorkshire and Humber as potential sites.

Friday's mini-budget comes after the Government announced an unprecedented multibillion-pound package to tackle sky-high energy bills and the cost of living squeeze.

Under the 'energy price guarantee', bills for the average household will go no higher than £2,500 at any point over the next two years. It will save a typical home around £1,000 a year from October 1, when the current consumer price cap had been set to rise, according to official estimates.

Businesses were promised similar levels of support, and Business Secretary Jacob Rees-Mogg is set to announce details on Wednesday.

With speculation building over the direction policy will take as Miss Truss seeks to put her stamp on No 10, it has also been suggested the PM could lift the ban on new grammar schools within months.

Chancellor plots 'rabbit out of hat' to tackle cost of living

Statement: Chancellor Kwasi Kwarteng will deliver his mini-budget on Friday

PM to tell UN we must curb Russia

By Chief Political Correspondent

LIZ Truss will tell world leaders this week that economic growth is key to facing down Russian aggression.

In a speech to the UN General Assembly, the Prime Minister will urge allies to end their reliance on imports of energy and other products from so-called malign actors.

She will say the West must learn lessons from Vladimir Putin's invasion of Ukraine by boosting economic security and defence.

A source told the Sunday Times: 'She will draw a clear link between geopolitics and the domestic economy (in particular energy prices), and why reducing the free world's dependence on malign actors has a direct impact on the cost of living and success of our economy here at home.'

In her address, she will also rally Western countries to help Ukraine in its push-back against Russian invaders.

Miss Truss is expected to fly to the summit in New York this evening, after attending the Queen's funeral. It will be her first overseas visit and major summit since she took office. Some 150 world leaders will attend. UN secretary general Antonio Guterres called for solutions to the world's divisions, which he said were 'the widest they have been since at least the Cold War'.

Miss Truss will also urge US President Joe Biden to stand firm against China's threat to 'freedom and democracy around the world'.

A source told The Mail on Sunday: 'Russia has demonstrated it's an acute, active threat to Western stability and prosperity, but Liz believes China represents the most serious long-term threat to our values and way of life.'

ANDREW PIERCE IS AWAY

Meanwhile, at the foot of the final left-hand news page, the Mail reports that Truss's new chief of staff, Mark Fullbrook, has been interviewed by the FBI as part of an election-rigging bribery investigation. It turns out that this is as a witness, not that he is suspected of any misconduct.

There will, however, soon be more controversy over the way he is to be paid. He is to invoice the PM through his lobbying company, rather than receive a salary as most people do – an arrangement that is reversed almost immediately after it is brought to light. Fullbrook also still owns 10% of another lobbying company he founded with the Australian Tory election guru Lynton Crosby, which may raise conflict of interest questions.

20 September

A politics-free day at last as the Mail devotes 79 pages of its 'historic souvenir edition' to the Queen's funeral.

For the first time in three days there is no photograph of Kwarteng in the paper. There were, however, plenty on social media after he was caught rocking with laughter while apparently taking a phone call in Westminster Abbey.

Any Labour chancellor, opposition backbencher, Tory Remainer or woke luvvie would, of course, have been given a similar free pass for such behaviour on such an occasion.

21 September

Daily Mail

WEDNESDAY, SEPTEMBER 21, 2022 Daily newspaper of the year 90p 55p to subscribers*

In a landmark speech, Liz Truss will link economic strength at home with standing up to authoritarian regimes abroad

FREEDOM BEGINS WITH TAX CUTS

From **Jason Groves** in New York

LIZ Truss last night signalled a tax revolution to try to boost flagging economic growth.

Speaking ahead of Friday's emergency Budget, she set out a bold agenda of tax cuts and regulatory reforms.

Sources said she wanted to lead Britain into a 'new era' – marrying freedom at home with stronger economic and security policies in an increasingly authoritarian world.

Tonight in New York the Prime Minister will urge Western leaders to follow suit, telling the UN General Assembly that economic reforms are needed to deal with the threat posed by Russia and China.

Yesterday she confirmed that Chancellor Kwasi Kwarteng will reverse the rise in national insurance and halt a planned hike in corporation tax. But she made clear that she was planning much broader tax cuts to make Britain more competitive.

Asked whether there was 'more to come' on tax, she replied: 'Lower taxes lead to economic growth, there is no doubt in my mind about that.' In an interview with the BBC, she added: 'We do have to take difficult decisions to get our economy right. We have to look at our tax rates.'

Her comments will fuel speculation that she intends to bring forward a planned cut in the basic rate of income tax, either this week or at a full Budget expected in November. The 1p cut is not due to be introduced until 2024 but Miss Truss and Mr Kwarteng are both said to view it as a way to ease the rising cost of living and boost growth.

In comments that echo the 1980s free market vision of Margaret Thatcher and Ronald Reagan, she will tell the UN: 'We want people

Turn to Page 4

Handshake: Emmanuel Macron with Liz Truss in New York last night

REVEALED: Simple – yet poignant – inscription for Queen's final resting place

SEE PAGES 6-7

Politicians get back to work and Truss gets back to the front page. This time in the company of friend-or-foe President Macron. For she is in New York for a UN meeting, where she will make a speech linking prosperity (to be created through tax cuts) with security. Inside, she is reported to be promising an increase in defence spending. The paper approves. Its leader says:

> *Having already unveiled a massive package to help families with soaring energy bills, she's now focusing her attention on growing the economy.*
>
> *The process will begin on Friday with a mini-Budget reversing the recent national insurance hike and scrapping planned corporation tax rises. There are reports she may go further by cutting income tax.*
>
> *These measures will put more money in people's pockets, create jobs, attract investment and fuel competitiveness. It's a bold and defiant start to her career as Prime Minister - and firmly rooted in traditional Conservative thinking.*
>
> *Some will say that cutting taxes will fuel inflation and drive up interest rates. But we already have the highest burden since the 1950s. The stale Treasury orthodoxies of the past two decades have failed miserably to deliver substantial growth.*
>
> *As Miss Truss will say: 'We want people to keep more of the money they earn. We believe that freedom trumps instruction.'*
>
> *It's an unashamedly Tory solution - and one that should make us all better off.*

A recurring theme is that the merit of Truss's strategy is that it is 'rooted in traditional Conservative thinking', that she is coming up with 'unashamedly Tory' solutions. At one point the fact that a policy of which the paper approves conforms to Tory ideology is described as 'the cherry on the cake'. It's almost as though it's such an unexpected bonus for a Conservative prime minister to come up with Conservative ideas that the fact has to be hammered home and applauded as an achievement in itself.

22 September

After desperate Kremlin leader warns West of Armageddon if he's thwarted on Ukraine, Liz Truss issues defiant riposte...

WE WON'T BE COWED BY PUTIN'S NUCLEAR THREATS

LIZ Truss last night warned Vladimir Putin he will never win in Ukraine despite his 'desperate' threat to use nuclear weapons.

She and Joe Biden both denounced the Russian despot

From **Jason Groves** in New York and **James Franey** in Brussels

in New York after he delivered a chilling speech in Moscow.

Putin said he had ordered the mobilisation of reserves to fight in Ukraine and claimed he was 'not bluffing' over the use of his nuclear arsenal. The crisis dominated talks between the Prime Minister and President Biden last night during which they insisted the West would not yield to aggression.

Addressing the UN general assembly in the early hours, Miss Truss said Putin was 'desperately trying to justify his catastrophic failures'.

She added: 'He is doubling down

Turn to Page 6

Truss at the UN makes the splash again, this time on her making defiant noises in Putin's direction.

Inside, a spread predicts that stamp duty will be cut and businesses given more help with energy bills in the 'massive' mini-budget on Friday, but 'gloomy analysts' warn that the 'gamble might not pay off' as interest rates are about to rise again.

Week 12

AT LAST! A PROPER TORY

23 September

Chancellor vows 'new era for Britain' as he unveils a massive package of measures to turbo-charge growth

BIGGEST TAX CUTS FOR 30 YEARS!

THE Chancellor will hail 'a new approach for a new era' of growth today as he unveils the biggest tax giveaway in three decades.

By **Harriet Line**
Chief Political Correspondent

Vowing to break a 'cycle of stagnation' that has lumbered Britain with a massive tax burden, Kwasi Kwarteng will outline action to support families and boost business.

His 'growth plan' has 30 measures to drive down taxation, tackle high energy bills and curb inflation. It includes cutting stamp duty, reversing the national insurance rise and scrapping a planned increase in corporation tax. Government sources suggested there might be a further 'rabbit out of the hat' announcement – possibly a 1p cut in the basic rate of income tax next year.

In other financial developments:

- The Bank of England yesterday hiked interest rates by 0.5 percentage points to 2.25 per cent – the highest level since 2008;
- It also declared that the economy was now shrinking but that a deep recession might be averted and inflation brought more under

Turn to Page 6

The excitement grows on the morning of the mini-budget (sorry, fiscal event), with a lead promising the biggest tax cuts for 30 years.

A TRUE TORY BUDGET

Top rate axed in bonfire of taxes

Chancellor springs surprise for earners paid over £150,000

How I'll win, by Dragons' Den star

'It will make Britain more competitive'

'As business grows, I will as well'

Penny off basic rate of tax will help 31m

'You cannot tax your way to prosperity'

WHAT THE TAX CHANGES MEAN FOR YOU

Great news, yet we need help now

Bankers' bonuses back to boost Britain

But millions still facing higher bills

The leader is fully behind the strategy, saying it will jolt the Tories into life:

> *Thankfully, the Chancellor and Prime Minister Liz Truss are determined to re-energise the country by taking a more radical approach - turbocharging growth.*
>
> *That is why the mini-Budget's centrepiece is the biggest tax giveaway since the 1980s. Mr Kwarteng will reverse the national insurance hike, scrap the planned rise in corporation tax and cut stamp duty.*
>
> *And a bonfire of red tape will unlock the shackles on business and accelerate crucial infrastructure projects.*

The editorial goes on to note that Nigel Lawson's tax-cutting budget helped Margaret Thatcher to win a third general election, and predicts similar good fortune for the Truss team:

> *There will, of course, be relentless shroud-waving from the Left and the BBC, who claim Mr Kwarteng's audacious agenda merely benefits the rich. But they are wrong, and he must stick doggedly to his guns.*

> *With the country heading into recession, we can't afford to surrender to the failed economic consensus. The Government must do all in its power to stimulate growth.*
>
> *If the country becomes more prosperous, everyone gets richer. And the Tories, too, will enjoy a political windfall.*

Oh, and the fracking moratorium has been lifted. This is in contravention of the 2019 manifesto pledge. The Mail has fought from the word go to get the national insurance rise reversed and repeatedly berated Sunak for breaking 'a solemn manifesto commitment'. When it comes to the return of fracking, of which the Mail approves, any mention of the manifesto is strangely absent.

24 September

Daily Mail

SATURDAY, SEPTEMBER 24, 2022

Daily newspaper of the year £1.30 90p to subscribers*

FREE INSIDE

Farewell Elizabeth the Great

MAGNIFICENT GLOSSY 48-PAGE MAGAZINE TO TREASURE

PLUS FREE

Queen Elizabeth II souvenir coin collection

For all new print subscribers

SEE PAGES 20-21 FOR DETAILS

*Minimum 3 months. Monthly payment will auto renew. Terms apply. See mailsubs.co.uk/coin

Top 45p tax rate scrapped and penny off income tax

Stamp duty slashed, rise in levies on beer & wine shelved

New dash for growth in biggest boost for 50 years

AT LAST! A <u>TRUE</u> TORY BUDGET

KWASI Kwarteng launched a £45billion dash for growth yesterday with the biggest tax cuts in half a century.

Unveiling a package that stunned MPs and financial markets, the new Chancellor

By Jason Groves Political Editor

slashed income tax and stamp duty, as well as pressing ahead with cuts to national insurance and corporation tax.

He said tax cuts were 'central to solving the riddle of growth' and set a target for boosting GDP after years of 'stagnation'. Business chiefs welcomed the measures, with the CBI saying there was 'no choice but to go for growth'.

Mr Kwarteng confirmed plans to reverse the increase in national insurance and halt a planned rise in corporation tax. But he also brought forward a planned 1p cut in income tax, taking the basic rate

Turn to Page 4

The Mail is overjoyed by Kwasi Kwarteng's package and celebrates with a splash head that has both an exclamation mark <u>and</u> an underscore. Inside spreads are upbeat with headings including 'Turbo boost to private firms', 'Stamp duty revolution' and 'Top rate axed in bonfire of taxes'.

A TRUE TORY BUDGET

Turbo boost to private firms

Rise in corporation tax is scrapped as Kwasi hands business £19bn 'to invest, to innovate and to grow'

'Investment zones' to cut tax and speed up planning

Round of applause as alcohol tax rises axed

Pub boss: It's still a crisis

Scan this QR code for a brilliant profile of Kwasi

VAT-free shopping for tourists

A TRUE TORY BUDGET

Top rate axed in bonfire of taxes

Chancellor springs surprise for earners paid over £150,000

How I'll win, by Dragons' Den star

Penny off basic rate of tax will help 31m

Great news, yet we need help now

Bankers' bonuses back to boost Britain

But millions still facing higher bills

A TRUE TORY BUDGET

Stamp duty revolution

No tax on properties worth up to £250,000 •• First-time buyers pay nothing below £425,000

'We missed out on the savings'

HENRY DEEDES

Tories greeted this course in Kwasinomics with a sonic boom of cheers

Genuine Tory Budget that spells end of Treasury doomsters

Guru who has Liz's ear

Alex Brummer says the budget will spell the end of Treasury doomsters, Daniel Johnson's Saturday essay describes Truss as the 'Brave, radical TRULY Tory prime minister no one saw coming',

Andrew Neil says it's a great gamble, but sticking with failed policies from the recent past would have been a greater one – and there's a chance the markets will soon be pleasantly surprised by how little extra borrowing is required.

Daily Mail

COMMENT

Tories gamble on new era of Trussonomics

The brave, radical, TRULY Tory PM no one saw coming

SATURDAY ESSAY by Daniel Johnson

What do you think of Liz so far? Scan here to vote in our The Mail+ poll

SCAN ME

Welcoming the era of Trussonomics – 'Tory in tooth and claw' – the leader also concedes it is a gamble, but a calculated one.

> *We can't yet know how well it will pay off. It requires the British people to play their part by increasing productivity in return for keeping more of their own money.*
>
> *But doing nothing is not an option. The economy is stagnating and in desperate need of a kick-start. Liz Truss and her Chancellor have produced a radical and intellectually coherent plan to achieve that. There is every sign it can work.*

The only spots of rain on the parade are the pound dipping and experts asking, back on page 18, 'how WILL Kwasi pay bill?'

26 September:

Daily Mail

FREE Queen Elizabeth II souvenir coin collection

FOR NEW PRINT SUBSCRIBERS: PAGES 16-17

MONDAY, SEPTEMBER 26, 2022 Daily newspaper of the year 90p 55p to subscribers*

Read this paper on your tablet or phone

£1 FOR THREE MONTHS

...or 12 months for £65

Subscribe at: mailsubs.co.uk

As Chancellor vows to defy critics and carry on cutting taxes...

KWASI'S BOOST FOR FAMILIES

The budget hasn't gone down as well with others – including Tory MPs – as it did with the Mail, and many are eyeing the opening of the markets this morning with trepidation. Not everyone thinks it's such a great idea to borrow billions of pounds to give back to the best-paid people in the country. Far from retreating, Kwarteng has spent the weekend promising that there are further tax cuts in the pipeline – characterised in the Mail splash as 'Kwasi's boost for families'.

A TRUE TORY BUDGET

'The British people will drive economy'

Truss may face revolt if pound drops below dollar, MPs warn

Increase to migration risks first Cabinet row

PM: Special relationship will be even more special

There are more of the chancellor's promises on the 6-7 spread, but all is not quite as joyous as hoped: MPs are warning Truss of a revolt if the pound drops below the dollar and there's a row brewing in Cabinet as Suella Braverman and Kemi Badenoch bridle at Truss's plans to increase immigration.

Further back, on pages 14 and 15, the Mail reports on the start of the Labour party conference under the head 'Labour turmoil on income tax'. This is because not all the big beasts agree.

It is already clear that not all Conservative MPs agree with Kwarteng's plans either. But there has, as yet, been no suggestion of 'Tory turmoil'.

27 September

Daily Mail

TUESDAY, SEPTEMBER 27, 2022 Daily newspaper of the year 90p 55p to subscribers*

PLUS New print subscribers get a FREE Queen coin collection

Subscribe today and get your Daily Mail... FOR ONLY 55p ...the same price as 10 years ago SUBSCRIBE AT: mailsubs.co.uk/coin

SEE PAGES 16-17

FURY AT THE CITY SLICKERS BETTING AGAINST UK PLC

Speculators profit from fall in pound ++ Sterling rallies on volatile day ++ Now fears of rate rise and mortgage pain

The markets still don't care for the budget; the pound is falling, the cost of borrowing is rising, mortgage deals are being withdrawn. The Mail homes in on who is to blame for this state of affairs in its splash: 'Fury at the City slickers'.

The 'fury' is coming from our old friends 'senior Tories', although just the one is quoted - 'veteran MP' Sir John Hayes. Another MP, Richard Drax, accuses the BBC of talking the pound down, but makes no mention of people profiting from it.

The speculating 'slickers' are a couple of hedge funds, one of which features again inside, where the paper also looks at two individuals known to have profited from the falling pound in the past – or at least to have advised people to bet against it.

One is Crispin Odey, a Tory donor (among other gifts, he contributed £10,000 to Boris Johnson's leadership campaign) who was also once

Kwarteng's boss. Two facts the paper does not mention. [As it turns out, he was apparently grouse shooting on his honeymoon rather than gambling on the markets over the weekend.]

'Making money out of bad news'

Q&A

City millionaires and the economic guru

Mortgage chaos as spooked lenders pull deals

Bank chief and Chancellor keep calm amid the currency turmoil

The leader, headlined 'There's every reason to believe in bold agenda', remains bullish:

> *To those who desperately want to see Kwasi Kwarteng's bold agenda for growth fail, the initial plunge represented a massive vote of no confidence by global investors. In truth, however, the equally rapid rebound suggested yesterday's early market volatility owed more to speculators trying to make a fast buck than any genuine verdict on the British economy...*
>
> *Mr Kwarteng delivered a coherent and ambitious Tory plan for growth. With a fair wind and a steady hand on the tiller, there is every reason to believe it can work. But it won't happen overnight.*

On the same page, the Mail's group business editor Ruth Sutherland reinforces the argument, saying the prime minister and chancellor must hold their nerve, concluding: 'The plan to jolt the economy back to health through tax cuts and reforms to free up business is the right — the only — recipe for long-term success.'

28 September

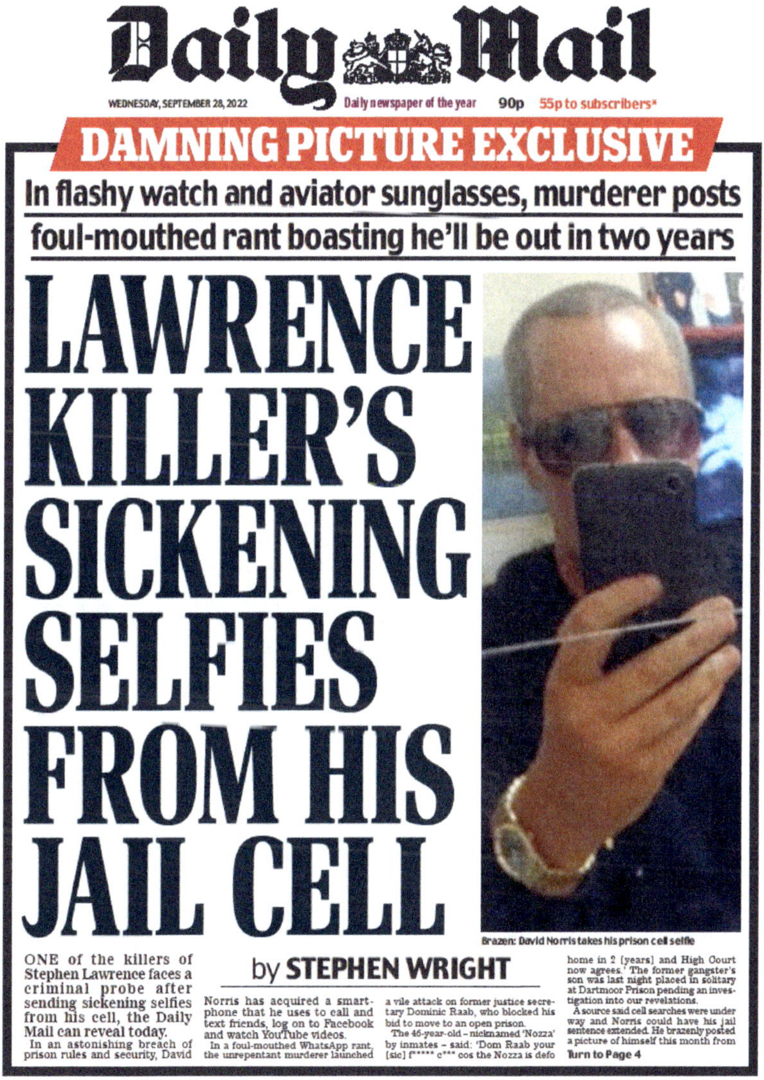

Daily Mail

WEDNESDAY, SEPTEMBER 28, 2022 Daily newspaper of the year 90p 55p to subscribers*

DAMNING PICTURE EXCLUSIVE

In flashy watch and aviator sunglasses, murderer posts foul-mouthed rant boasting he'll be out in two years

LAWRENCE KILLER'S SICKENING SELFIES FROM HIS JAIL CELL

Brazen: David Norris takes his prison cell selfie

by STEPHEN WRIGHT

ONE of the killers of Stephen Lawrence faces a criminal probe after sending sickening selfies from his cell, the Daily Mail can reveal today.

In an astonishing breach of prison rules and security, David Norris has acquired a smartphone that he uses to call and text friends, log on to Facebook and watch YouTube videos.

In a foul-mouthed WhatsApp rant, the unrepentant murderer launched a vile attack on former justice secretary Dominic Raab, who blocked his bid to move to an open prison.

The 46-year-old – nicknamed 'Nozza' by inmates – said: 'Dom Raab your [sic] f***** c*** cos the Nozza is defo home in 2 [years] and High Court now agrees.' The former gangster's son was last night placed in solitary at Dartmoor Prison pending an investigation into our revelations.

A source said cell searches were under way and Norris could have his jail sentence extended. He brazenly posted a picture of himself this month from

Turn to Page 4

The alarm on international markets at Britain's direction of travel continues. The IMF tells Truss to reverse the tax cuts; mortgage lenders are withdrawing more products and raising rates for new loans; the i reports that senior officials had warned the chancellor and prime minister that their plans would lead to market turmoil, but that they had been determined to press ahead. Meanwhile, Keir Starmer addresses his party conference.

These developments provide the lead story for all but three national papers: the Star (asteroid blasted by Nasa), the Express (get your flu and Covid jabs) – and the Mail, which has spotted a squirrel over there. This takes the form of Stephen Lawrence's killer having a mobile phone in jail. This is so dramatic that it warrants the entire page being put in a black border with a white-on-red 'Damning picture exclusive' label.

The Labour conference makes the 8-9 spread – 'Is Keir plotting a Lib-Lab pact?' – while the economy is relegated to pages 14 and 15, where the paper reports '284 deals pulled in mortgage panic'. This spread tells the IMF to 'butt out' and accuses the Bank of England of being 'asleep on the job'.

It also returns to Crispin Odey, reporting on his claim that 'bitter Remainers' in the City were responsible for the run on the pound. This time it does mention his links to Kwarteng.

284 deals pulled in mortgage panic

Lenders remove top offers as bank websites crash and homeowners brace for another interest rate hike

Q&A

Bank chief has been 'asleep on the job', say angry Tories

Flaccid and muddled

'The gifts that keep on giving'

Hedge fund tycoon's shameless boasts over his lucrative bets against UK plc

Liz really is put through her paces

Butt out of Britain's affairs, IMF told

On the OpEd page, Alex Brummer continues the attack on Andrew Bailey, accusing him of a 'muddled and flaccid' response to the growing crisis.

Meanwhile, in the world of silver linings, Money Mail asks 'Will Kwasi's stamp duty cut stave off house price crash?'

29 September

The Bank of England spends £65bn buying government debt to protect pension funds as the fallout from the budget continues, ministers are contemplating billions of pounds of public spending cuts, but the prime minister is nowhere to be seen. All this makes the lead for every paper, including the Star, Express and pro-budget Telegraph, which has an above-the-titlepiece puff urging Truss to hold her nerve.

Daily Mail

THURSDAY, SEPTEMBER 29, 2022 Daily newspaper of the year 90p 55p to subscribers*

FINANCIAL MARKETS TURMOIL

Bank steps in to soothe the City's jitters | Ministers urge calm and insist no policy U-turn | Were risky pension trades behind chaos?

SEE PAGES 8-12

PRISON X-RAY FINDS PHONE HIDDEN IN LAWRENCE KILLER'S BODY

EXCLUSIVE

by STEPHEN WRIGHT

THE smartphone used illegally by one of Stephen Lawrence's killers in his prison cell has been found inside his body after he was X-rayed at Dartmoor prison.

Officials discovered the device after investigating the Daily Mail's bombshell revelations that David Norris, 46, had used it to send messages and selfies to friends outside.

Specialist scanning equipment located the black smartphone in an intimate place after this newspaper tipped off the Ministry of Justice that Norris had been flouting strict prison rules.

Staff raided Norris's cell on Tuesday evening while he was elsewhere. After failing to find the phone, they X-rayed him and the scanner revealed a 'large rectangle object' – later confirmed to be a smartphone.

Hours later, the phone was seized and is set to be examined by the Prison Service's digital investigations unit to establish who the

Turn to Page 5

Kate, la belle de Paris! SEE PAGE THREE

Every paper, that is, except the Mail, which is still preoccupied with its squirrel with a mobile phone. And Kate Moss.

The economic turmoil does, however, make the top of the front, having been completely absent yesterday.

Billions in cuts to calm the markets

Defiant ministers' radical spending plans in bid to restore stability

'Unprecedented volatility in all developed markets'

'Trying to soothe the City'

Is new risky type of trading by pension funds behind chaos?

'A sudden cash call of over £100million'

Keep 45p tax rate, jittery Tories tell Kwasi

And there are two spreads inside. One asks if a new kind of pension fund trading is behind the chaos, the other has 'senior Tories' blasting the IMF, saying its warning had wreaked havoc. Two are quoted: John Redwood and Lord Frost.

Tories blast IMF after warning wreaks havoc

'They will plunge us into recession'

COMMENTARY by Alex Brummer

How can such risky trading be happening all over again?

Homeowners panic over fears of timebomb for mortgages

'The market is a car crash'

Q&A

Young family's dream of a bigger home is fading fast

Scan this QR code to say how you'd vote in a general election tomorrow

In the OpEd, Matthew Lesh says that the IMF specialises in posturing and getting things wrong. A few pages on, Stephen Glover still likes Kwarteng, but says he needs to 'wise up'. The problem lies not with the Truss-Kwarteng policies, but the way they are selling them.

The leader – 'Jittery Tories risk fuelling market misery' – still believes in the 'bold low-tax, pro-growth mini budget' and is casting around for people and organisations to castigate, starting with the IMF and the Bank of England, as well as 'advocates of the failed economic consensus, Remainers refighting the Brexit battles of 2016 and a hysterical anti-Tory media'.

Even so, it is becoming concerned about Truss and Kwarteng's presentational skills, saying they are not easing jitters by going missing while the crisis rages. It is also becoming concerned that they are not getting the loyalty from their colleagues the paper expects – there are already murmurings that they should go. The Mail is having none of it. After all, those MPs are back in their favourite pub:

> *Some Tory MPs are so twitchy that they have intimated the PM and Chancellor should quit - less than a month in post.*
>
> *But that would be suicidal. With Labour streets ahead in the polls, the Tories are drinking in the last-chance saloon.*
>
> *Changing the leader is not an option. The project was never going to yield overnight results, so they have got to get behind it. Voters will never forgive internecine warfare when they face financial misery.*

Week 13

A VOLLEY OF HURRAHS

30 September

Daily Mail
FRIDAY, SEPTEMBER 30, 2022 Daily newspaper of the year 90p 55p to subscribers*

Queen died of old age at 3:10pm. But Harry wasn't told for over three hours

SEE PAGE FIVE

■ Panicking Tory MPs call for U-turn on mini-Budget tax cuts

■ Bombshell poll gives Labour a 33-point lead

■ But Kwasi and the PM insist going for growth IS right plan

TRUSS: I'M NOT FOR TURNING

Liz Truss emerges from hiding to take part in a series of local radio interviews that prove not to be the easy ride she might have hoped. Labour is now 33 points ahead in the polls, Tory MPs are 'reeling', with some demanding a rethink – or at least for the chancellor to show his workings – but Truss insists that she is sticking to her plans.

This makes the splash for the Mail, turning to page 6, where the headline is 'Rebels told they risk handing victory to Labour'. This message is from a truly unbiased source – the chancellor, who has also 'broken cover' – and is reinforced by a full-page comment piece by Daniel Hannan saying the prime minister must not back down.

ECONOMY TURMOIL

Tory rebels told they risk handing victory to Labour

Kwarteng: I won't scrap the pension triple lock

Truss is doing the right thing. If she backs down now, it's an admission no meaningful reform can ever be undertaken

COMMENTARY By Lord Hannan

The less we pay in tax, the more we can spend

This will be the beginning of real prosperity

On the next spread, Guy Adams investigates the 'real scandal' of reckless financiers gambling with our pensions.

ECONOMY TURMOIL

Perfect storm as lenders pull mortgages and sales collapse

Ex-Bank chief Carney attacks Truss over 'unfunded' £45billion tax cuts

Guy Adams INVESTIGATES

Is the real scandal that reckless financiers were able to risk so much of our pensions in what very nearly became...

A £1.5 TRILLION DEATH SPIRAL

History teaches us nobody will be held to account

Stark warning over investments was ignored

Volatility vortex led to funds essentially eating themselves

The leader, 'Defending bold tax plans is Tory duty', is also concerned about recklessness – and for the first time Truss is in the line of fire. It was reckless, the paper says, for her to bury her head in the sand when the public expected reassurance. Her silence was baffling. But she still had the right strategy, she must keep going and everyone else must catch up.

The fact is, there has been a rabid overreaction to Chancellor Kwasi Kwarteng's blueprint to turbocharge growth.

Miss Truss rightly believes that by growing the size of the pie, everyone can enjoy a bigger slice... by deviating from the globalist consensus, Miss Truss has had the flame thrower turned upon her.

Yet the whole world is in economic turmoil and on the brink of going into recession. It's entirely plausible that the PM and Mr Kwarteng are ahead of the game by trying to boost growth with tax cuts - and may save us from the worst of any downturn.

So Tory MPs must shake off the delirium gripping them. That the one truly Conservative fiscal policy introduced in the past 12 years has caused such panic shows what an utter shower many are.

Some are said to have already submitted letters of no confidence in the new PM. If true, this is nothing short of insanity.

They must simply buck up and get behind Miss Truss.

1 October

The search for the body of Moors murder victim Keith Bennett is front-page news and the economy is relegated to pages 14 and 15, with the 'good news' being that Britain is neither in recession nor the sick man of Europe.

ECONOMY TURMOIL

At last some good news, we are not in recession!

Here comes the 50-year mortgage

Get repeat savings on your pet's favourite food

with easy-repeat

30%

Kwasi's emergency talks with watchdog

Tories threaten rebellion over 45p tax rate axe

The data shows UK is no 'sick man of Europe'

Alex Brummer's ANALYSIS

New energy bills price cap from today

ANDREW NEIL

The IMF killed Labour. Black Wednesday did for Major. Will KamiKwasi budget be the end of Truss?

By last summer, it was clear inflation was here to stay

Labour's poll lead is possibly unassailable

If you're an outlier in the current financial climate, the markets will have you for breakfast

But the Mail's pundits are beginning to voice doubts. Andrew Neil writes that with the global economy flooded with cheap money, you could see why Truss and Kwarteng might have thought they could borrow to fund tax cuts and stimulate the economy – but they hadn't taken into account the return of inflation.

More experienced hands, including Sunak, realised that was a game-changer, he continues. But Truss and Kwarteng were guilty of a 'massive and unforgiveable miscalculation' when the return of inflation was there for all with eyes to see.

The headline on Neil's column dares to ask 'Will Kamikwazi budget be the end of Truss'. The leader – 'Don't be turkeys, stick with Liz' – sincerely hopes not. It is still with the programme:

> *The Government is right not to U-turn on the controversial mini-Budget. Leave aside that to do so would be a catastrophe, leaving Miss Truss's authority in tatters.*
>
> *In fact, the policies - from protecting firms and families from ruinous energy bills to one of the biggest tax giveaways in history - are commendable. And, crucially, defendable.*
>
> *So it's vital Miss Truss puts the communication failures behind her. With the right messaging, she can reassure the public and markets that she will jolt our sclerotic economy back to life responsibly, and that everyone will ultimately be better off.*

3 October

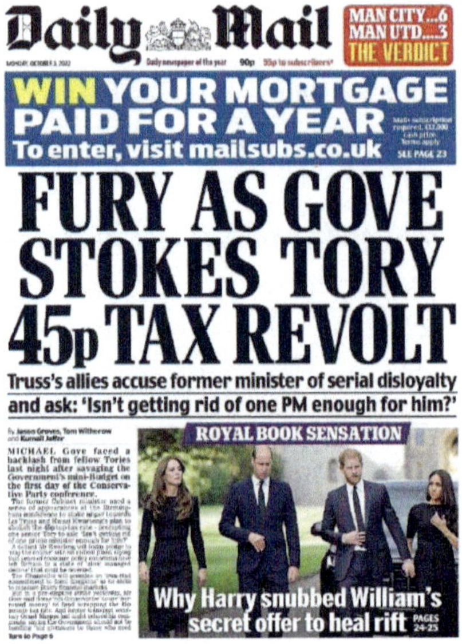

Daily Mail

MAN CITY...6
MAN UTD...3
THE VERDICT

WIN YOUR MORTGAGE PAID FOR A YEAR
To enter, visit mailsubs.co.uk

FURY AS GOVE STOKES TORY 45p TAX REVOLT

Truss's allies accuse former minister of serial disloyalty and ask: 'Isn't getting rid of one PM enough for him?'

ROYAL BOOK SENSATION

Why Harry snubbed William's secret offer to heal rift PAGES 24-25

Daily Mail

MAN CITY...6
MAN UTD...3
THE VERDICT

WIN YOUR MORTGAGE PAID FOR A YEAR
To enter, visit mailsubs.co.uk

As two ex-ministers lead mounting revolt and Whitehall insider tells Mail row is 'distracting' from mini-Budget's benefits...

ARE TORIES ON BRINK OF 45p TAX U-TURN?

ROYAL BOOK SENSATION

Why Harry snubbed William's secret offer to heal rift PAGES 24-25

The Conservatives have gathered in Birmingham. In a pre-conference interview with Laura Kuenssberg, Liz Truss had maintained that while she had 'failed to prepare the ground' properly for the mini-budget, there would be no reversal on the 45p tax rate.

But by the time Mail goes to press, she is clearly wobbling and it switches its splash headline from 'fury' at Michael Gove for 'stoking revolt' to 'Are Tories on brink of U turn?'

The text doesn't change much, though. There's no fury in evidence, but Gove is said to have 'sparked a backlash' by saying that cutting the top tax rate 'displayed the wrong values' and 'senior Tories' are warning him that he is damaging the party.

In this case there's just the one – Iain Duncan Smith, who obliges with a rather wonderful soundbite: 'It's Sunday, the first day of conference for a new Tory leader and Michael Gove is out there stabbing her in the back. Isn't getting rid of one prime minister enough for him? Someone needs to confiscate his knives – he is a danger to people and to the party.'

CONSERVATIVES IN BIRMINGHAM

Truss: I failed to prepare ground for mini-Budget

HENRY DEEDES SKETCH

Zoik! The screen went dead on the Liz 'n' Laura show

Naked criticism of the new PM did not land well...

Analysis By Jason Groves

There does, however, seem to be quite a backlash against the abolition of the 45p rate, with 'a string of Sunak-supporting MPs' speaking out against it – and Grant Shapps describing it in The Times as a 'politically tin-eared cut'.

CONSERVATIVES IN BIRMINGHAM

Kwasi: We'll get Britain booming

Chancellor adamant his plan is only way to stop UK's 'managed decline'

COMMENTARY by Daniel Johnson

Ditch the grenades Michael, unity is essential

Kwarteng, who will be first up in front of the party faithful, trails his speech with a promise to 'get Britain booming', making the first inside spread. The second goes to the Truss TV interview.

The leader – 'Disunited Tories will reap electoral disaster' - says the prime minister and chancellor were right to admit to mistakes, but they should stay the course and their party should back them.

> *Trussonomics is a breath of fresh air, blowing away the cobwebs of the failed economic orthodoxy. Defibrillating the sluggish economy will turbocharge growth, incentivise hard work, increase wages and bring in more money for public services.*
>
> *After years of politicians who change their minds with the wind, it is refreshing to have leaders who believe being right is more important than being popular.*
>
> *To show that the Tories are competent though, it is imperative MPs get behind Miss Truss - and not just to stab her in the back.*

4 October

By Jason Groves, Harriet Line and Kumail Jaffer

LIZ Truss was under fire from senior Tories last night for caving in over tax cuts.

Her shock decision to abandon plans to scrap the top rate of income tax alarmed supporters worried about her determination to pursue the rest of her radical programme.

'I know I said I'd watch it but I'm doing a U-turn'

The Prime Minister's critics, including Michael Gove, seized on the climbdown over the 45p rate and immediately started targeting other parts of her agenda, such as capping a rise in benefit payments.

'Her position is such that she really can't afford to make any more mistakes,' said a former minister who backed her leadership

Turn to Page 2

Screeching late-night reversal on tax policy they vowed they'd stick to ++ Threat of new revolt on benefits ++ As Truss refuses to rule out more U-turns, despairing Tories tell PM...

GET A GRIP!

The 45p tax rate is restored, Kwarteng is 'clinging on', and the Mail has seven pages on the U-turn, starting with a splash telling the PM to get a grip.

There's a sketch on the chancellor's conference address at which perspiration was 'seeping from his forehead like Niagara Falls'.

CONSERVATIVES IN BIRMINGHAM

Kwasi clings on after 'owning' 45p debacle

He admits to 'tough day' as revolt eases

New U-turn on date of next mini-Budget

HENRY DEEDES SKETCH

Perspiration seeped from his forehead faster than water crashing down Niagara Falls

Dorries: PM should go to polls to win a mandate

Another climbdown by the Treasury

'If this lot are off their sausages, it's time to sound the alarm'

LITTLEJOHN

Andrew Pierce is drafted in for one of his colour efforts describing the late-night crisis meeting in a Hyatt hotel room where the decision to reverse ferret was reached. And Andrew Neil pronounces the dream of low taxes to be dead in a ditch.

CONSERVATIVES IN BIRMINGHAM

She'll face down rebels over £7bn benefits row

'I hope the lesson is well learnt'

And it's a turnaround for the pound too after 45p furore

The late-night crisis meeting in Liz's 22nd floor Hyatt suite where the lady decided she WAS for turning

Andrew Pierce reporting

ARE TORIES ON BRINK OF 45p TAX U-TURN?

'She knew that the U-turn was going to cost her'

'They have used up a lot of goodwill'

For all that, the Mail is still convinced that Truss is on the right path and the leader – 'No more buckling on dash for growth, PM' – seeks to stiffen her resolve:

> *It is imperative Miss Truss holds her nerve on her radical agenda, which rejects the failed high-tax, low-growth consensus and aims to adrenalize our atrophying economy, creating jobs and prosperity.*
>
> *The reality is, Miss Truss's policies are the only hope of avoiding a Labour government. Yet the rebels seem to hate her more than they fear Sir Keir Starmer and his Left-wing cranks seizing power.*

5 October

Daily Mail

WEDNESDAY, OCTOBER 5, 2022

Daily newspaper of the year 90p 55p to subscribers*

Get our Mail+ app £1 for 3 months mailsubs.co.uk

Truss has broken the first rule of politics. Keep your friends close but your enemies (like my ex-husband) even closer

SARAH VINE SEE PAGE 17

Truss pledge: Stand by my approach and we will ALL benefit

By Jason Groves Political Editor

Civil war for Tories

'No more drift and delay'

The Mail looks away from the economy to splash on a promise that police will attend every burglary (do we really believe that?), but Sarah Vine has some advice for the PM in her column that is deemed worthy of front-page billing. Essentially, it's 'don't trust Michael Gove'.

Page 2 previews Truss's speech to conference – 'stand by me and we will ALL benefit' – but the spreads further back tell a different story, with 'Tory chaos and civil war' and more Kwarteng U-turns.

CONSERVATIVES IN BIRMINGHAM

Tory chaos on day of civil war

- Suella raps Gove and Co for 45p tax 'coup'
- Cabinet bigwigs slam PM's threat to welfare
- New Kwasi muddle over next mini-Budget

Ministers in open revolt against the benefits squeeze

'So many b*****ds are trying to block Liz'

Dorries: Boris wants warring MPs to back Truss and save the party

On the OpEd, Arthur Laffer, the 82-year-old American economist who gave his name to the 'Laffer curve' showing that reducing tax rates can increase revenue, says he is dismayed by the 45p reversal, while the leader – 'First speech, new start' – confronts the possibility that this could be Truss's one and only conference address as leader:

> *It is a sign of the delirium gripping the Tories that Liz Truss's first conference speech as Prime Minister could be her last.*
>
> *Miss Truss understands perfectly that Britain's prosperity depends on urgently jump-starting our lethargic economy.*
>
> *We wish her well today. We'd like nothing more than to hear a rousing, visionary speech that re-imposes her authority, silences dissenters, and starts a new chapter for her premiership - and the country.*

6 October

Daily Mail

THURSDAY, OCTOBER 6, 2022 Daily newspaper of the year 90p 55p to subscribers*

'Tory malcontents have a choice: Get behind Truss... or consign their party to oblivion and despatch Britain into the ruinous clutches of Starmer'

DAILY MAIL COMMENT SEE PAGE 16

What's the secret weapon Kate shared with PM? PAGE FIVE

DEFIANT LIZ TAKES FIGHT TO HER CRITICS

After tempestuous 12 days she rouses Tories by vowing to defeat the enemies of growth holding Britain — and working people — back

By Jason Groves and David Churchill

LIZ Truss vowed to take on the 'enemies of enterprise' yesterday.

Shrugging off Tory infighting, she spelt out an upbeat vision of a 'new Britain' in a combative speech to the Tory conference.

The Prime Minister pledged to break up an 'anti-growth coalition' of vested interests, Brexit deniers and the Left 'holding the country back'.

She said she was determined to navigate a way through the cost of living 'tempest' and 'put us on a stronger footing as a nation'. Using the word 'growth' 27 times, she admitted her plans would cause disruption but there was 'no alternative' if Britain wanted to return to prosperity.

To reassure the money markets she hinted at spending cuts and promised 'iron discipline' with the public purse.

Her speech, which was interrupted by environmental protesters, was designed as a riposte to her critics and to reset her premiership after 12 bruising days of U-turns and astonishing

Turn to Page 2

Truss delivers her speech and the Mail is happier. Sketchwriter Henry Deedes is withering about her delivery – 'Truss's jokes can be clunky and her timing as off as a month-old carton of whipping cream' – but he says that this is a woman who doesn't give up and proclaims the speech a triumph: 'a pugnacious pinger, delivered with aplomb'.

CONSERVATIVES IN BIRMINGHAM

Liz pledges to defeat anti-growth coalition

She resets her Premiership with optimistic vision – and a dig at her critics

HENRY DEEDES SKETCH

Expectations were low, but the PM exited to a volley of hurrahs

GETTING BRITAIN MOVING

Johnson a better bet as leader, says poll

Who'd make the best Tory leader? Scan this QR code to vote

Truss out of tune with M People

The headline notes that she left the stage to a 'volley of hurrahs'. A rather muted manifestation of a 'triumph', given that Truss was talking to the very people who had just elected her. (In defiance of the majority of MPs, who preferred Sunak – and only because they couldn't have Johnson.)

This is, after all, a showpiece event where standing ovations for the leader are noted for their longevity: Thatcher was rewarded with one lasting six minutes for her 'the lady's not for turning' speech in 1980. That's quite a long time to stand and clap and whoop – try it.

Rather like GCSE results, there followed a period of ovation inflation, so that by 1987, when she secured her hat-trick of election wins, delegates were on their feet for eleven minutes.

A 'volley of hurrahs' isn't quite in the same league.

On the next spread, Daniel Johnson sees a Truss who is less awkward, more confident and wonders if this could be the turning point, but a little further on Stephen Glover fears the 'surprisingly good speech' won't be enough.

CONSERVATIVES IN BIRMINGHAM

Unite behind PM or lose election, rebel MPs told

Liz shrugs off the 'anti-growth' activists

'Meet the needs of the nation'

COMMENTARY by Daniel Johnson

Less awkward, a bold vision. Could this be a turning point?

Now for a rendezvous with Macron

The leader – 'PM's speech should cool rebel hotheads' – also sees signs of hope, and says the address proves she is the best option for leader. Recalcitrant Tory MPs should stop whingeing – a point it is so eager to get across that it flags it up in blue at the top of page 1.

> *She will never have Boris Johnson's flair for working an audience. But... her address was strong, reassuring, authoritative and, above all, a ringing endorsement of Tory values.*
>
> *In a defiant cri de coeur, she laid out a coherent, compelling and exciting true blue vision for Britain. A place where aspiration, enterprise and prosperity triumph over the tyranny of low expectations...*
>
> *Miss Truss's speech proves she's still the best option as leader. If she's dethroned, it will surely trigger a snap election.*
>
> *The Conservative malcontents destabilising her have a simple choice. Get behind the PM and help lift up the nation.*
>
> *Or persevere with their self-indulgent troublemaking and consign their party to electoral oblivion - and the country to the ruinous socialist clutches of Keir Starmer.*

SHE'S MADE A PIG'S EAR OF IT

7 October

With the conference over, there should be a couple of days of calm before Parliament gets back to work next week. Yet Tory MPs – and even members of the government – are restless.

Ministers warn Liz: No more 'unforced errors'

By Jason Groves
Political Editor

CABINET ministers have warned Liz Truss and Kwasi Kwarteng to end the 'unforced errors' that wrecked the Conservative Party's annual conference.

'We've been kept in the dark'

£43,750 for Maggie the masterpiece

The Mail seems to have had its fill of the Conservatives for a while, since they go AWOL from the front for an entire week. But on page 14, a page dominated by a true Tory heroine who was definitely not for turning, political editor Jason Groves says they are warning Truss and Kwarteng to get their act together. His report takes as read that the conference had been 'wrecked' and that the mini-budget the paper is so keen on had been 'botched'.

Ministers are speaking out after being excluded from budget planning and there is already another row brewing – over whether benefits should rise in line with wages – around 3% - or inflation, which is running at about 10%.

8 October

Daily Mail

COMMENT

Stop the plotting and unite behind the PM

Diabetes breakthrough

Don't abuse power

Defiance and revenge have replaced loyalty, unity and good sense

By bungling the introduction of their growth agenda, the Prime Minister and her Chancellor may have killed off the chance of historic Tory reform for a generation, says ANDREW NEIL... and it's a tragedy

SATURDAY ESSAY by Andrew Neil

HUMBLING OF THE RADICALS

It all promises to be very messy indeed

Tory backbenchers know that the Government is discredited

There are still rumblings about rebellions on fracking and now Truss and Mogg are seen to be at odds about whether there should be an energy-saving ad campaign.

Other Mail writers may have felt some hope after the Truss conference address, but Andrew Neil describes her as having 'got through' a workmanlike speech and concludes that she left the gathering in worse shape than when she arrived – having arrived in 'very poor shape indeed'.

His Saturday essay senses that the end is near, not only for Truss, but for the Conservatives as the party of government:

> *There is a palpable fin-de-siecle mood in the Tory parliamentary party these days. Infighting, plotting, defiance, self-interest, revenge – these have all replaced unity, loyalty, good sense and the national interest among so many Tory MPs, many of whom seemed to have lost the plot.*
>
> *It was quite remarkable how many senior Tories in Birmingham rushed, off the record, to say how awful Truss was.*
>
> *These are all common features of a governing party that is coming to the end of its life – that has lost the will to rule and is more interested*

> *in its own internal tribal rivalries than the good government of the nation.*
>
> *That is the real, ghastly legacy of Birmingham for Truss. It will haunt her for the weeks and months to come.*

Neil goes on to describe the budget as 'calamitous' and says Truss and Kwarteng, 'through a lethal combination of inexperience and stupidity, have managed to kill off the chances of genuine, radical Tory reform for a generation'. They are now meek and muted, totally in thrall to the 'institutions of financial orthodoxy'.

On the same page, however, the leader – 'Stop the plotting and unite behind PM' – still sees the best in Truss and believes that she can yet turn things round, if only Tory MPs would get into line.

> *Liz Truss's make-or-break conference speech...was largely well received. Markets have recovered. Dissenters, for now, have been stilled.*
>
> *Meanwhile, on the international front, the Prime Minister demonstrated deft diplomacy during her trip to Prague on Thursday where she and Emmanuel Macron agreed to step up efforts to smash the evil gangs enabling the Channel crossings.*
>
> *There are grounds, too, for optimism over the troublesome Northern Ireland Protocol.*
>
> *With these positives in mind, there is no reason to believe that when Parliament returns from recess on Tuesday, Miss Truss cannot recapture the cavalier spirit of her leadership campaign and get back to her bold, tax-cutting economic agenda.*
>
> *Given the terrifying alternative which awaits the country come the next election, Tory MPs must be duty bound to put away their squabbles and unite behind her.*

10 October

After a weekend that saw four cabinet ministers writing newspaper columns urging their backbenchers to unite behind Truss, the prime minister starts inviting groups of them to lunches and receptions at No 10, which makes the splash for some and an inside spread for the Mail.

Liz launches her charm offensive

Truss to meet restive MPs as she tries to get her premiership back on track

Zahawi: We must plan for blackouts ... even though they're unlikely

But will she do another U-turn amid storm over benefit rate?

Now Labour says it WILL reverse tax cut

Sacked minister is set for knighthood

Anger at Sturgeon's 'I detest Tories' outburst

The leader writers get a break from Tory infighting, but on the OpEd, Dominic Lawson backs Mogg over Truss saying the government SHOULD be telling us how to save energy.

11 October

Kwarteng is obliged to bring forward his budget statement from next month to October 31, when he is expected to publish the OBR's assessment of his measures and to announce deep spending cuts.

Page 10 — Daily Mail, Tuesday, October 11, 2022

Prepare for Kwasi's Halloween Budget

Chancellor told to slash public spending by £60bn

By Jason Groves
Political Editor

KWASI Kwarteng will have to slash public spending by £60 billion to bring government borrowing under control, a report warns today.

In a fresh U-turn yesterday, the Chancellor announced he will rush forward a major economic statement designed to show he is serious about tackling the Government's towering debts.

The so-called 'medium-term fiscal plan' will now be published on October 31, just days before the Bank of England meets on November 3 to discuss a possible big rise in interest rates.

But despite the Halloween Budget, government borrowing costs continued to rise yesterday.

Today's report by the Institute for Fiscal Studies (IFS) warns that Mr Kwarteng may have to cut spending in most departments by 15 per cent to balance the books.

'Trimming the fat will not be enough'

It says this would require cuts totalling more than £60 billion – and questions if the Government has the capacity to drive through spending restraint on this scale, saying it risks 'stretching credulity to breaking point'.

The IFS report finds that increasing benefits in line with earnings rather than inflation could raise £13 billion, while cuts to investment spending might raise a further £14 billion. But with the NHS and defence budgets protected, other departments would still face deep cuts, because 'trimming the fat' will not be enough to fill the hole in the public finances.

IFS director Paul Johnson said it was 'just about possible' that Mr Kwarteng would be able to get debt falling in five years. But he warned that pencilling in 'unspecified tax cuts' for later years would undermine his credibility. With ministers already struggling to persuade Tory MPs of the need to squeeze the welfare bill, Mr Kwarteng faces a race to identify potential cuts in time.

One Whitehall source said: 'It is obvious to everyone that there are going to be some very tough decisions.' Another said government departments were likely to be asked to operate within their existing budgets for now, with deeper cuts likely to be pencilled in only after the next election.

Commons Treasury committee chairman Mel Stride welcomed Mr Kwarteng's decision to hold a Halloween Budget, saying the plan may result in a smaller rise in interest rates, which was 'critical to millions' of mortgage holders.

But he warned this would be the case only if the plan 'lands well with the markets' ahead of the Bank's decision. Asked whether Mr Kwarteng's financial plans added up, Mr Stride said: 'well, we're about to find out'.

Today's IFS report predicts that government borrowing will now hit almost £200 billion this year – double the £99 billion that was forecast at the time of the last budget in March.

Meanwhile, an analysis by investment bank Citi forecast the economy was set to grow by an average of just 0.8 per cent a year for the next five years – far short of the 2.5 per cent rate of growth the Chancellor said he wants to achieve.

The Treasury has said Mr Kwarteng's plans will pay for themselves if they succeed in raising economic growth by 1 per cent above its forecast level.

But he now faces a battle to persuade the Office for Budget Responsibility that a series of supply side reforms in areas such as planning, energy and immigration will turbocharge growth.

Former Treasury mandarin Lord Macpherson said the scale of the fiscal challenge could force the Chancellor to revisit his tax-cutting plans. The crossbench peer said: 'Unless the Government can restore economic credibility, the market response in the weeks ahead could be a whole lot worse than we have seen so far.'

Comment – Page 16

Liz Truss and England defender Lucy Bronze hold the Euro trophy yesterday as the PM met the Lionesses for the first time

'I can't watch – It's too scary!'

PM blocks Kwarteng job choice

LIZ Truss yesterday blocked Kwasi Kwarteng's plan to appoint an outsider as the Treasury's top official.

The Chancellor had been poised to install high-flying civil servant Antonia Romeo as the permanent secretary as part of plans to shake up the department's 'orthodox' thinking.

Mr Kwarteng sacked the previous incumbent Sir Tom Scholar on his first day in office last month as he tried to force the Treasury to take a bolder approach to growth.

But Whitehall sources said the appointment of Mrs Romeo was overruled by the PM. Instead, civil service veteran and 'fiscal conservative' James Bowler was appointed yesterday.

Two other senior Treasury officials – Cat Little and Beth Russell – were appointed as Mr Bowler's deputies in an apparent bid to reassure the financial markets of fiscal responsibility.

No10 yesterday insisted that Mr Bowler's appointment had been a 'joint decision' between the PM and Chancellor.

Solar on the back burner

THE Prime Minister vehemently opposes placing solar panels on farmland due to Britain's increasing 'food security issue', No10 confirmed last night.

Liz Truss – who has previously warned against the 'blight' of solar farms on the countryside – wants to strike 'the right balance' between renewable energy production and maintaining 'productive' farmland, Downing Street said.

It comes after reports that Environment Secretary Ranil Jayawardena is reforming agricultural planning laws to curb the development of solar power.

A Department for Environment, Food and Rural Affairs spokesman said: 'We are committed to increasing our long-term energy security and strengthening the UK's food security.'

The leader – 'Time for a fresh start' – says that now is the opportunity for Tories to consign their febrile conference to history and push the reset button.

> *Supporting Liz Truss's bold growth agenda, and so making families and businesses better off, is the only way the Conservatives can turn around their pitiful poll ratings and avoid annihilation come the election...After a dreadful month, the Tories must now show unity, discipline, clarity of message and leadership. A divided party will simply hand the keys of No 10 to Labour - with all the misery that will entail.*

12 October

Daily Mail

Get our Mail+ app £1 for 3 months mailsubs.co.uk

WEDNESDAY, OCTOBER 12, 2022 Daily newspaper of the year 90p 55p to subscribers*

As she dies aged 96, how Angela Lansbury became one of TV's richest women

SEE PAGES 24-25

MPs' plea as Palace sets May 6 as date for Charles III's crowning

NOW MOVE BANK HOLIDAY FOR THE CORONATION!

Parliament returns with Kwarteng straight into the firing line with Treasury questions. While he is defending his budget, the Bank of England says it can't afford to keep bailing out pension funds and that it will stop intervening on Friday, sending the pound into reverse.

There are now suggestions that Truss will, after all, impose some kind of windfall tax on energy companies or at least cap their profits. The Times, Guardian, Telegraph, FT, and i front pages all focus on the economy, but the Mail (in common with the Express) is more interested in the coronation next spring and the death of Angela Lansbury.

The Guardian

Power giants to face windfall tax after all as Truss delivers U-turn

i

Truss bids to silence rebels with cap on energy profits

The Daily Telegraph

Sterling falls as Bank pulls plug on pension help

THE TIMES

Threat to pensions as Bank cuts its support

Plunging Pound fury at bank chief

He comes under fire after saying pension funds won't get more help

POUND V DOLLAR YESTERDAY

Alex Brummer

First day back – and how Kwasi wished he could be anywhere else

Don't try to penny pinch on benefits, Kwarteng warned by Rishi's allies

'Ministers will canvass opinion widely'

Rees-Mogg plans £15billion raid on renewable energy

HENRY DEEDES SKETCH

IMF upbeat on UK growth

An inside news spread again casts the Bank of England as villain, while on the OpEd, Alex Brummer blames the 'presentation' of the budget, with its unfunded tax cuts, for the chaos that has rocked the gilts market.

The leader – 'Global turmoil' – also accepts that the budget was 'mishandled', but says the whole world is suffering – and turns its fire on the BBC and 'the Left':

> *Listening to the shrieks of the Left and the BBC, one might think the Government's mishandled mini-Budget had single-handedly crashed the economy.*
>
> *Yes, it caused a temporary slump in the pound. Yes, interest rates are back to historically typical levels. And yes, we face pain from high energy prices and inflation.*
>
> *As Liz Truss warns, the economic outlook is gloomier than at any time since the financial crash. But while the immediate future is bleak, the UK is not alone in this turmoil. The entire world is suffering a hangover from lockdown and Russia's war.*

13 October

Truss is back in the Commons for PMQs, but the real story is happening in the markets, which are on the slide again as the Bank's cut-off point approaches. So Truss v Starmer takes a back seat to a spread on the 'dithering Bank' and 'flip-flopping' Andrew Bailey, where Alex Brummer is again raging at the 'gaffe-prone' governor.

Dithering Bank rattles markets

Bailey accused of flip-flop on emergency bonds bailout

Key blunders that led to slump in the pound

June 2022

September 2022

May 2021

October 2022

How long till they ask: Who can rid us of this gaffe-prone governor?

from Alex Brummer

Recession fear as economy shrinks

Brexit pique fuels Economist's Truss hatred

Andrew Pierce reporting

There is also irritation with the Economist over a leader calling Truss 'The Iceberg Lady' – because she had the 'shelf life of a lettuce'*. Andrew Pierce describes this as a 'vicious attack' that shows how the 'arch-Remainer' magazine has given up all pretence of political balance. He then embarks on a quick runaround of its history and Italian ownership, its contempt for the Conservatives and its 'Brexit pique'.

The leader writers are cross both with the Bank and Tory MPs.

The first leader says the 'bungling Bank' must invest in UK stability; the second – 'Malcontents' mayhem' – replays a familiar theme:

Liz Truss's dash for growth is already limping badly after she made a pig's ear of presenting her ambitious mini-Budget and was forced into humiliating U-turns.

She is, however, severely hamstrung by Tory rebels.

Miss Truss's plan, which sticks to Conservative principles, is the right one - and they should get behind it. The truth is, it is the only conceivable way the Tories can avoid impending electoral oblivion.

[Electoral oblivion is another good one to have on the bingo card.]

**The lettuce analogy may have angered the Mail, but it appealed to the Daily Star, which would pick up and run with the idea over the coming days – to the point of setting up a live stream of a lettuce to see whether it would outlast Truss. It did. To celebrate, perhaps goading the Mail, it published an 'historic souvenir edition' and moved on to portraying Boris Johnson as an aubergine. The stunt won the Star – which never acknowledged where the idea had originated – publicity all over the world. Yet the Mail never found it necessary to commission its consultant editor to write a column criticising the Reach newspaper group, the publishers of this more widely-seen version of the same insult.*

Page 14

Daily Mail, Thursday, October 13, 2022

Daily Mail

COMMENT

Bungling Bank must invest in UK stability

Malcontents' mayhem

A study in intolerance

Arrest, don't indulge!

Just 37 days after taking power, Liz Truss is a prisoner of her own MPs and unable to do pretty much anything...

TRUSSED UP!

by Stephen Glover

COLUMNS about politics usually define a problem and propose a solution. This time it's different. I don't really see any way out for Liz Truss.

Kibosh

Pressure

The rebels in her party — or the markets — could force Liz Truss to climb down

The Mail leadership now seems to be adrift from its star columnists. For on the same page, Stephen Glover follows Andrew Neil in concluding that it's looking bad for Truss. He agrees with the leader writers that she is trapped by her own party, a virtual captive, unable to do what she wants – trussed up, in fact. But he can see no way out for her, beyond hoping that outside forces will make things better.

> *Has there ever been a Prime Minister new to the job so hemmed in on every front? In her abject powerlessness she is like a leader who has been in office for years and has run out of options and support. But she has only just started! And she has a majority of nearly 70.*

Week 15

HER AUTHORITY IS SHOT

14 October

PM 'HAS 17 DAYS TO SAVE HER JOB'

By **Jason Groves**
Political Editor

MPs turn on troubled Truss in mini-Budget debacle as 'senior Tories line up Sunak and Mordaunt'

MUTINOUS Conservative MPs have given Liz Truss 17 days to save her job.

Tory whips warned she could face a leadership challenge if Kwasi Kwarteng's economic statement on October 31 fails to end the turbulence in the financial markets.

And late last night it was reported that Rishi Sunak and Penny Mordaunt were being lined up on a joint ticket to replace the Prime Minister.

Senior Tories are preparing the pair, who both ran in summer's leadership contest, to enter No10 if the current Prime Minister falls, according to The Times. The Prime Minister and her closest aides were last night weighing up whether to ditch parts of last month's emergency mini-Budget, including her flagship pledge to scrap an £18billion hike in corporation tax.

Asked about the prospect of another humiliating U-turn, the Chancellor said yesterday: 'Let's see.' It comes as panicked Tory MPs engaged in fevered discussions about whether to try to remove Miss Truss barely a month into her premiership – and who might

Turn to Page 2

For all the Mail's cajoling, Tory MPs are still plotting and reportedly eyeing a Sunak-Mordaunt dream ticket. Everything, it seems, will hinge on the chancellor's statement on October 31 and whether that calms the markets – and the party.

The Mail splashes that the PM has 17 days to save her job, speculates inside about another U-turn – this time on corporation tax – and allows its political editor to contemplate a Sunak or even Johnson premiership.

Business tax... the next U-turn?

Kwarteng says he WILL keep job but he hints at more back-tracking

OUT?

OUT?

IN?

IN?

So what happens now... and could Rishi (or even Boris) come back?

Truss told: Don't drop reform of care funds for elderly

The leader, 'Liz Truss must turn things round – fast', is still in her corner – just – and it really, really doesn't want a change of leadership. So much so that it comes up with a truly great variant on its leader bingo card 'turkeys voting for Christmas'.

> *If the markets remain spooked, heaping mortgage and pensions misery on millions, and Labour are still out of sight in the polls, Miss Truss's enemies in Conservative parliamentary party will surely act.*
>
> *They should think twice. If they did strike, it wouldn't just be like turkeys voting for Christmas, but switching on the oven and peeling the potatoes too.*
>
> *Tory MPs need to remember they are there to deliver Boris Johnson's 2019 manifesto which gave them their biggest majority in half a lifetime.*
>
> *If they don't and instead try to install a new leader, it will be chaos - even more so than now (if such a thing is possible).*

15 October

Daily Mail

SATURDAY, OCTOBER 15, 2022 Daily newspaper of the year £1.30 90p to subscribers*

EAT TO BEAT THE MENOPAUSE

Lots of broccoli and blueberries but NO white bread – an expert guide to change your life SEE PAGES 36-38

After another day of barely believable Tory chaos...

HOW MUCH MORE CAN SHE (AND THE REST OF US) TAKE?

Strain: Liz Truss making her emergency statement yesterday

HER first 38 days in office have proved some of the most shambolic in British political history.

But yesterday – Liz Truss's 39th day in Downing Street – saw the

By Jason Groves, David Churchill and Kumail Jaffer

chaos, confusion and flip-flopping reach extraordinary new extremes.

To the astonishment of Westminster and beyond, she abandoned her flagship cuts to corporation tax and brutally sacked her friend and Chancellor Kwasi Kwarteng – all in a bid to save her failing premiership.

Miss Truss said the moves, which tore the heart out of her plans for boosting growth, would reassure jittery financial markets about the state of the public finances. But last night senior Tories continued to voice doubts about whether the PM could stay in power.

Some ministers are already holding informal talks with senior backbenchers about the possibility of installing a new leader by 'consensus'. One said: 'If this is going to work we need to make it

Turn to Page 2

Kwarteng is summoned back from key international meetings in Washington to be sacked – hours after telling the BBC's Faisal Islam 'I'm going nowhere'. Jeremy Hunt is rushed in as chancellor and promptly junks most of the budget, including the cut in corporation tax.

Truss calls a press conference to announce the changes at No 11, but looks all at sea and allows only four questions, giving the same answer each time and declining invitations to offer any apology or express any regret.

HOW MUCH MORE CAN WE TAKE?

Political turmoil hits the pound yet again

Liz Truss deserves all she gets

Things must change for Tories - and fast
COMMENT: PAGE 19

ANDREW NEIL has been a Truss sceptic from the start. Now, after another disastrous day that saw another humiliating U-turn, he says the radical tax-cutting agenda is dead in the water for a generation

GAME, SET AND MATCH TO THE BLOB

by Andrew Neil

She has reduced British politics to absurdity

I find it hard to see how she can survive as PM

After weeks of blaming the Left, the markets, the Bank of England, Putin and restless Tory MPs in defence of its woman, the Mail splash is brutal:

> *Her first 38 days in office have proved some of the most shambolic in British political history.*
>
> *But yesterday - Liz Truss's 39th day in Downing Street - saw the chaos, confusion and flip-flopping reach extraordinary new extremes.*
>
> *To the astonishment of Westminster and beyond, she abandoned her flagship cuts to corporation tax and brutally sacked her friend and Chancellor Kwasi Kwarteng - all in a bid to save her failing premiership.*

Inside there are seven news pages, including space for Sarah Vine and Andrew Neil. Vine is exasperated by the press conference and the prime minister's failure to show her human side; Neil, described as 'a Truss sceptic from the start', says that any hope of a radical tax agenda is dead for a generation.

HOW MUCH MORE CAN WE TAKE?

Poppadom plot to oust the PM

Rebel MPs seek new leader to avert Tory 'wipeout'

KEY FIGURES WHO MAY DECIDE HER FATE

SARAH VINE

View from the sofa

Why couldn't she just say something human, from the heart? What a missed opportunity

We got robot Liz, a flat refusal to accept any blame for the mess

A full-page leader, however, defends the paper's view that Truss was the right choice for prime minister and that her strategy was right. It nevertheless concedes that her time in office has been a disaster and asks how sacking the chancellor for implementing her own policy makes sense.

If things don't change – and lightning fast – the day will come for the grown-ups in the Tory party to take charge...

Daily Mail COMMENT

The person who first wields the blade often quickly becomes a victim

Surely there are people of good sense who'll put the country first

First, though, it reminds readers that it never wanted a change of leadership in the first place. Boris Johnson was a winner, a man of stature and magnetism, levered out of office by lesser colleagues over essentially trivial misdemeanours.

To their lasting shame, those Tory MPs were now paying a bitter price. Thanks to them, the country was forced to endure a bitter and unedifying leadership race as MPs indulged in wild surges of enthusiasm for one candidate after another, followed by equally capricious switches of allegiance.

In the end, they passed the decision to that great unknown, the Tory Party membership, all too easily dismissed as unrepresentative and out of touch. They chose Liz Truss.

The Mail supported that choice...alas, nobody can pretend that Ms Truss's few frantic weeks in Downing Street have fulfilled the promise she seemed to show. On the contrary, it is impossible to argue that her premiership thus far has been anything other than a disaster.

Even Liz Truss's most loyal allies, viewing the matter through the most rose-tinted glasses available, must now wonder how she can survive. Yet what is the alternative? Another interminable leadership election of the sort we have just endured would be impossible, and might come up with an answer just as misguided as it provided the first time around.

Where there's life there's hope and, of course, it's still just possible that Truss, one of the Tory party's great survivors, may pull off some kind of miracle recovery.

But if she doesn't get her act together – and lightning fast – the message will surely spread throughout the Tory party that the only conceivable hope of winning the next election lies in an intelligent, swift and universally accepted resolution of this crisis.

Having spent the previous three months first urging MPs members to install Truss in office and then railing at the behaviour of those same MPs, the Mail now asks if there aren't 'in our governing party' some 'men and women of judgment and sense with the best interests of the country at heart'. The day may come, it concludes, for them to assert themselves and for the 'grown-ups' to take charge.

Quite who these grown-ups are, the Mail does not explain. The MPs the paper encouraged readers to vote for at the last election? The MPs who – rightly in the Mail's book – backed her agenda? The MPs who – wrongly in the Mail's book - questioned that agenda? Or is there a mystery supply of grown-ups lurking among the parliamentary Tory party who have yet to play any part in this drama?

17 October

Daily Mail

MONDAY, OCTOBER 17, 2022 Daily newspaper of the year 90p 55p to subscribers*

FREE LIMITED EDITION

Queen Elizabeth II

TEA TOWEL

SEE PAGE 43

When you sign up to The Mail+ app at mailsubs.co.uk

ONLY £1 FOR THREE MONTHS

ELIZABETH II

First MPs go public with calls to quit ++ Rebels push for 1922 chairman to step in ++ But PM's allies warn ousting her will only trigger election

PLOT TO TOPPLE TRUSS THIS WEEK

The 'plotters' are now coming out of the woodwork, with MPs openly calling on Truss to quit. Hunt seems to be running the government and Ben Wallace is piling on the pressure over defence spending.

On the OpEd, Dominic Lawson is the latest columnist to turn on Truss, saying that Margaret Thatcher would never have risked her agenda of massive unfunded tax cuts.

HOW MUCH MORE CAN WE TAKE?

Amid speculation Defence Secretary could be a 'unity candidate'...

Wallace issues ultimatum to Truss over her defence pledge

Javid 'victim of four-letter No10 slur'

'It is not a discretionary spend but a priority'

Welby: No moral case for tax cuts for the wealthiest

Should Truss quit? Scan this QR code to vote in our exclusive poll

70% of The Mail+ readers say that PM should quit

by Paul Bracchi

He once foiled IRA bombers. Now could he unite warring Tory factions?

Influential website abandons Liz

The leader is still calling for unity though, for the first time, not necessarily behind Truss. But there's a warning that if those crazy MPs dump her, they'd better be ready to go to the country.

> *Tory enemies are exploiting the economic turmoil to plot her downfall, with three backbenchers calling on her to quit. Cabinet ministers are also manoeuvring.*
>
> *Whatever happens this week, they need instead to show unity and clarity of purpose. Millions struggling with soaring household bills will not forgive the Tories indulging in another bout of infighting.*
>
> *If they think voters will easily accept the party installing another PM without a general election, they're misguided.*

18 October

Daily Mail

TUESDAY, OCTOBER 18, 2022 | Daily newspaper of the year | 90p | 55p to subscribers*

FREE LIMITED EDITION
Queen Elizabeth II
TEA TOWEL
SEE PAGE 18

Available to first 10,000 new subscribers only. Terms apply

When you sign up to The Mail+ app at mailsubs.co.uk

ONLY £1 FOR THREE MONTHS

ELIZABETH II

■ Truss finally says 'sorry' for errors in painful TV mea culpa

■ She's reduced to spectator as Hunt tears up her mini-Budget

■ PM tries to rally her MPs – but 1922 chief warns many want her to quit

IN OFFICE, BUT NOT IN POWER

By **Jason Groves** Political Editor

LIZ Truss was last night warned she was 'in office but not in power' as she issued a grovelling apology for blunders on the economy.

Speaking after new Chancellor Jeremy Hunt dismantled her tax-cutting growth plans, the Prime Minister acknowledged she had gone 'too far and too fast'.

COMMENT

IT'S time for the wise men and women of the Conservative Party to decide whether the loss of confidence in Miss Truss is terminal. If it is, they must come to a solution – and fast – that can command the support of MPs and the millions of Tory voters looking on in horror.

SEE PAGE 16

'I want to accept responsibility and say sorry for the mistakes that have been made,' she told the BBC. 'I was expecting it to be tough and it has been tough, I think it's fair to say.'

Earlier, Mr Hunt used an extraordinary five-minute televised statement to axe 'almost all' of the Prime Minister's flagship tax cuts in

Turn to Page 2

HAUNTED PM LEAVES WESTMINSTER LAST NIGHT

Showing the strain: Liz Truss is driven away from Parliament

Truss gives an interview to Chris Mason of the BBC, apologising for going 'too far, too fast' with her economic reforms. Asked if she will lead the party into the next election, she says she will. But that looks unlikely, even to the Mail.

HOW MUCH MORE CAN WE TAKE?

I am sorry, Liz finally admits

In dramatic BBC interview, Truss 'accepts responsibility' for mini-Budget turmoil... and opens up on pain of sacking Kwarteng

HENRY DEEDES SKETCH

No, the PM's NOT hiding under a desk, said Penny

Let me fight on - PM's desperate appeal to MPs

HOW MUCH MORE CAN WE TAKE?

HUNT SHREDS TRUSSONOMICS

New Chancellor axes swathes of PM's economic programme by scrapping her tax cuts and clawing back £32bn for the Treasury

WHAT HE DITCHED FROM THE MINI-BUDGET...

POLICY	CHANGE	RAISED
Corporation tax		£18.7bn
Income tax		£5.9bn
Dividends		£900m
45p rate		£2.1bn
Tax-free shopping		£2.1bn
Self-employed		£2bn
Alcohol		£600m
	TOTAL	£32.3bn

...AND WHAT HE HAS KEPT

		COST
National insurance		£15.2bn
Stamp duty		£1.7bn
Bankers' bonuses		£0
Annual investment allowance		£1.3bn
	TOTAL	£18.2bn

FROM TORY WET...

TO PM IN ALL BUT NAME

The spirit of adventure has been smashed on the rocks of austerity

COMMENTARY by Alex Brummer

Advisory council 'restores orthodoxy'

Alex Brummer is dismayed that Trussonomics have been shredded by Jeremy Hunt, and Stephen Glover is angry that her 'ill-judged actions' have set back the cause of a low-tax economy by a decade or more and almost certainly handed the keys of No 10 to Keir Starmer.

Richard Littlejohn asks: 'When just shy of 14 million of us handed PM Boris Johnson an 80-seat majority, did anyone seriously suggest what we really wanted was Jeremy Hunt running the country?'

Then again, he continues, who could have imagined that Tory MPs would 'hound Boris from office and install Liz Truss?' His newspaper had repeatedly raised the first half of that question – but Littlejohn seems oblivious of its role in securing the second half.

And, anyway, Tory MPs didn't want Truss, they wanted Sunak.

The leader finally recognises that her days are numbered, but still manages an 'if' in its headline 'If PM is a lame duck, wise Tories must act'.

> *It promised to usher in a golden era of prosperity for all, rich and poor, with a laserlike focus on igniting the lethargic economy.*
>
> *But yesterday, after the most disastrous month for Tory politics perhaps since the Suez crisis, a stake was driven through the heart of Trussonomics.*
>
> *Her authority and credibility are as good as shot.*
>
> *The mini-Budget was the right thing to do in principle and contained many perfectly reasonable, defendable measures...But the execution was so ham-fisted it rattled the markets, triggering a damaging economic chain reaction - including a rise in mortgage costs - for which the Government may never be forgiven...*
>
> *By lurching from crisis to self-inflicted crisis, the Conservatives risk irrevocable damage to the party, its electoral fortunes and, as a result, the whole country.*
>
> *It's time for the wise men and women of the Conservative party to decide whether the loss of confidence in Miss Truss is terminal. If it is, they must come to a solution – and fast.*

Once again, it offers no clue as to who these wise men and women are. Surely not the 'plotters' who decided a week or more ago that Truss should go?

19 October

MILLIONS FACING PAIN ON PENSIONS

Retirees set to miss out on up to £430 a year as No10 signals it's ready to axe 'triple lock'

MILLIONS of pensioners could face an income squeeze of up to £430 next year after Liz Truss ditched her pledge to protect the 'triple lock'.

In a surprise U-turn, Downing Street warned she was no longer committed to raising pensions in line with inflation, despite having guaranteed just that only two weeks ago.

It said the Prime Minister was now

By **Jason Groves** and **David Churchill**

'not making any commitments on individual policy areas' ahead of the Halloween Budget – when ministers need to find £40billion in cuts.

One option being considered by the Treasury is for pensions to rise in line with earnings rather than inflation, meaning an increase of 5.5 per cent instead of 10 per cent.

That would cost pensioners £8.35 a week, or £424 a year, but save around £4.5billion a year, according to the Institute for Fiscal Studies. The proposal sparked an immediate backlash, with Age UK warning of a 'betrayal of our older population'.

Tory MP Nigel Mills said it was 'ridiculous' not to keep the triple lock, which guarantees that the state pension will rise in line with either inflation, earnings or 2.5 per cent – whichever is the highest. He warned the move could cost the party at the next election because so many older people vote Tory.

'The idea that people on a fixed income would not get an increase in line with inflation is preposterous,'

Turn to Page 6

Having told Tory MPs yesterday that they must act fast, the Mail now wants 'a period of calm' until the budget statement promised for October 31. But there is fresh wrangling as Downing Street says the 'triple lock' that guarantees pensions will at least rise with inflation may be ditched – two weeks after the prime minister said she was committed to the increase.

A poll suggests that most party members want Truss out, with Johnson favourite to come back, but some are calling for her to be given time to try to turn things round.

HOW MUCH MORE CAN WE TAKE?

Poll: Majority of Tory members want her out

And survey finds Boris would be their favourite as replacement

WHAT THE PARTY FAITHFUL THINK

Scan this QR code to vote in The Mail+ on who should lead the country

The Mail+ poll: Johnson for PM

Liz retreats over defence cuts after ministers threaten to quit

'One thing I'm sure of – she'll go'

'Will hold her to pledges she's made'

Truss texted Hunt to offer him No11, but he thought it was a prank and ignored her

Andrew Pierce reporting

THE DASH BACK FROM BELGIUM

On the OpEd page, Christopher Snowden says that to blame Truss and Kwarteng for the economic turmoil is 'fake news', a 'short-sighted and cynical narrative peddled by the BBC and the Left'. The mini-Budget didn't crash the economy, it had crashed long before she took office, as a result of two decades of over-borrowing. And worse is to come, whoever is in power.

The leader – 'Find a unity candidate or oblivion beckons' – has still not quite given up on its woman, although it notes that Jeremy Hunt is now effectively running the country and asks who gave him a mandate.

> *There's no doubt Liz Truss has been severely wounded by the events of recent weeks. If she is to survive, she must rediscover some of the fight and fire she showed during the leadership hustings.*
>
> *But the party must also be cautious of trying to oust her now, before any credible alternative has been worked out.*

Sarah Vine is more forthright. For her, Truss's game is well and truly up. She likens the appointment of Jeremy Hunt to 'ordering rump steak on your Ocado shop and finding they've replaced it with a tofu burger', says there is no such thing as a 'unity candidate' and blames the entire mess on Sunak – which he should now be made to clear up.

After the events of the past few days, the fact that Liz Truss is still pretending to be Prime Minister might seem to many not just absurd, but bordering on the deranged.

She hasn't just made a fool of herself: she's made fools of all those who voted Conservative at the last election. In a few short weeks, she has turned the party of Churchill and Thatcher into a laughing stock — and pretty much guaranteed a Labour landslide at the next election.

Whatever the Tories do now, the chances of winning a new mandate, let alone the kind of majority that Boris Johnson delivered in 2019, seem less than zero.

There is no 'unity candidate', no one person who can appease all the factions. That's just pie in the sky. Everyone — from Rishi Sunak to Penny Mordaunt to Ben Wallace — represents a red line to someone. The only way the Tories can undo that damage is to put a grown-up in charge. Someone who is a known quantity, however imperfect. What we need now is a purely bureaucratic solution, dull predictability instead of pyrotechnics.

If it were up to me, I'd choose Rishi Sunak. Not because I think he's the best man for the job (or because my ex-husband has told me to: strange as it may seem, I do occasionally have opinions of my own). It's because he's the one who got us into this mess in the first place by pushing out Boris.

If he hadn't resigned, Boris would still be in No 10. Instead, we have this shambles. And ultimately, it's Sunak's fault.

20 October

Daily Mail

THURSDAY, OCTOBER 20, 2022 Daily newspaper of the year 90p 55p to subscribers*

FREE LIMITED EDITION
Queen Elizabeth II
TEA TOWEL
SEE PAGE 28
When you sign up to The Mail+ app at mailsubs.co.uk
ONLY £1 FOR THREE MONTHS

Braverman quits as Home Secretary then plunges knife into PM ++ Shapps replaces her... despite plotting against Truss ++ Chief Whip 'resigns' amid chaotic late night vote ++ And the final astonishing revelation...

SUELLA'S 90-MINUTE SHOUTING MATCH WITH LIZ

By Jason Groves, Harriet Line and Martin Beckford

LIZ Truss's premiership was in freefall last night.

In an astonishing few hours, she sacked Suella Braverman after a 90-minute 'shouting match' – and then saw her Chief Whip 'resign'.

The ousted Home Secretary launched an outspoken attack on the PM, accusing her of breaking key pledges and wobbling over manifesto commitments such as reduced migration.

Chief Whip Wendy Morton and her deputy Craig Whittaker appeared to quit after Miss Truss reversed her plan to expel Tory MPs who voted against the Government on fracking.

No10 was last night unable to say whether it still had a chief whip.

Amid chaotic scenes in the Commons, Deputy Prime Minister Therese Coffey and Business Secretary Jacob Rees-Mogg were accused of 'manhandling' MPs through the voting lobbies – a claim both ministers denied.

As Government discipline collapsed, Mr Whittaker was heard telling his colleagues: 'I am f***ing furious and I

Turn to Page 2

Suella Braverman quits (or is sacked) as Home Secretary, ostensibly for breaking the ministerial code, and sends an absolute zinger of a resignation letter, saying that the business of government relies on people accepting responsibility for their mistakes. 'Pretending we haven't made mistakes, carrying on as if everyone can't see them, and hoping that things will magically come right is not serious politics.'

The whips resign, then unresign over confusion about whether a fracking vote was a confidence issue. Grant Shapps is appointed to succeed Braverman and, among its three inside spreads, the Mail reports that the cabinet has been captured by 'left-wingers', with Andrew Pierce back on patrol to report that three of the four great offices of state are now held by people who voted Remain.

The leader – 'The wheels have come off the Tory clown car' – makes almost the same point. Although it chooses to forget that Truss voted to stay in the EU and instead homes in on two of those offices being held by 'Remain-supporting centrist technocrats'.

The Mail has finally given up on the Truss premiership. It's just a question now of whether she can or should survive until the budget statement at the end of the month:

> *Of course, it may be sensible to let Miss Truss take the brickbats until after the Halloween Budget, when her botched mini-budget will be buried in ignominy.*
>
> *But if things don't soon turn around, surely wise party chiefs must begin arbitrating between the warring factions to alight on a unity candidate to replace her.*
>
> *The country, facing demanding challenges, is crying out for strong leadership. Not a Government mired in mayhem, fragility and acting with ever more political expediency.*

Week 16

HURRAH FOR OUR RISHI!

21 October

Daily Mail

FRIDAY, OCTOBER 21, 2022 Daily newspaper of the year 90p 55p to subscribers*

TORIES IN MELTDOWN

UNRIVALLED REPORTS & ANALYSIS PAGES 2-15

Truss was a disastrous dalliance who served only to remind us what a real leader looks like

SARAH VINE PAGES 2-3

As PM quits in ignominy after 44 tumultuous days, it's set to be...

BORIS v RISHI: FIGHT FOR SOUL OF THE TORIES

By Jason Groves, Harriet Line and David Churchill

BORIS Johnson and Rishi Sunak led the race to succeed Liz Truss last night after she became the shortest-serving Prime Minister in history.

After a disastrous 44 days in office she quit when party chiefs told her she had lost the confidence of Tory MPs.

The Prime Minister, who had abandoned her economic plans in the face of market turmoil, said: 'I cannot deliver the mandate on which I was elected.'

Her sudden departure triggered a frantic scramble to find a successor – with party chiefs ruling the contest should be over in a week. Candidates will need the backing of 100 Tory MPs by 2pm on Monday to take part in the contest – five times the threshold set for the last contest.

Last night no candidates had formally declared but Mr Johnson and Mr Sunak were racing ahead in terms of nominations – setting up a potential clash between allies turned bitter rivals.

A close political ally of the former PM last night said he was 'rested', 'in great spirits' and 'itching to take the fight to Keir Starmer'.

A close ally of Mr Sunak said there would be a 'natural logic' to him facing off against Mr Johnson, adding: 'It will be a battle for the soul of the party.'

The ex-chancellor last night had

Turn to Page 2

Allies turned rivals: Boris Johnson and Rishi Sunak are the favourites to become prime minister

And then she was gone. The king across the water is threatening to return and the Mail foresees a Boris v Rishi 'fight for the soul of the Tory party' (which is exactly what it called Liz v Rishi back in the day). In a big blue puff at the top of the front, Sarah Vine describes Truss as a 'disastrous dalliance' and, across the 2-3 spread, writes about her being delusional and of her resignation speech showing 'Trumpian levels of dysfunction and denial'.

FIGHT FOR SOUL OF THE TORIES

Her speech showed Trumpian levels of dysfunction and denial... rarely have I felt such fury

Sarah Vine

Failing to show contrition was the cherry on the cake

Vanity and lust for power drove her to mislead

In full, Liz Truss's Downing St statement

I CAME into office at a time of great economic and international instability. Families and businesses were worried about how to pay their bills. Putin's illegal war in Ukraine threatens the security of our whole continent. And our country had been held back for too long by low economic growth. I was elected by the Conservative Party with a mandate to change this. We delivered on energy bills and on cutting national insurance.

And we set out a vision for a low-tax, high-growth economy – that would take advantage of the freedoms of Brexit.

I recognise though, given the situation, I cannot deliver the mandate on which I was elected by the Conservative Party.

I have therefore spoken to His Majesty the King to notify him that I am resigning as leader of the Conservative Party.

This morning I met the chairman of the 1922 Committee, Sir Graham Brady. We have agreed that there will be a leadership election to be completed within the next week. This will ensure we remain on a path to deliver our fiscal plans and maintain our country's economic stability and national security.

I will remain as Prime Minister until a successor has been chosen.

Thank you.

She comes out on top... as shortest-serving PM

This is just the start of 15 pages of 'unrivalled reports and analysis' on the 'Tories in meltdown'. The next spread is all about Johnson: he is 'itching' to unite the party and take on Starmer and, if his prospects look good, might cut short his holiday in the Caribbean. Mick Hume writes that only he can stop the Conservative party turning into a Blairite blancmange.

Sunak, 'the man whose resignation triggered Boris's downfall', is the obvious favourite, and he is on the next left-hander having a think. 'Woke' Mordaunt is above him, with some anonymous MPs warning other anonymous MPs not to back her because of her views on trans rights.

Under a headline that asks a question it has already itself answered: 'Bookies make Sunak odds-on favourite...but who'd bet against Boris?', Andrew Pierce springs into action again on the next page, going through the potential candidates. Sunak is 8/11, Johnson 10/3.

FIGHT FOR SOUL OF THE TORIES

Boris loyalists: Bring him back

Weeks after being forced out of No10, Johnson's allies say he is 'itching to take the fight to Starmer' and re-unite party

100 backers needed by Monday, so will it even go to a vote?

How leader will be chosen

Only Johnson can stop Tories turning into a Blairite blancmange

COMMENTARY By Mick Hume

Of Sunak, Pierce writes that he 'goes into this race as front-runner thanks – at least in part – to his refusal to play to the gallery on tax cuts. His dismissal of Truss's policies as "fairytale economics" now looks extremely prescient.'

A cruel person might remind the Daily Mail of its July 22 headline 'Tax cuts aren't a fairytale, Rishi!'

After another spread, on the 'PM's agonising 24 hours as her fate was sealed', Tories are dismissing calls for an immediate election, while Richard Littlejohn sees the whole thing as a palace coup by Remainers. He asks 'What would possess any party to elect a new leader and then jettison her six weeks later?' and then answers his own question: 'In the event, Truss imploded under self-inflicted pressure', adding, 'But if MPs didn't want her as Prime Minister, they shouldn't have put her in the final two to go before the membership in the first place.'

But his paper told them to. Over and over again.

We then have a picture spread on the 'shortest and most turbulent premiership in our history'. Daniel Johnson concludes that Truss's problem was all down to bad timing. It was the decision to launch a radical new growth plan in the week of the Queen's funeral that proved fatal. Neither the country nor the markets were ready for the package she and Kwarteng 'sprang upon the world'.

FIGHT FOR SOUL OF THE TORIES

Awake all night... texts to friends at 4am... PM's agonising 24 hours in No 10 as her fate was sealed

With a Mona Lisa smile she left to face life as a pub quiz answer

HENRY DEEDES

SKETCH

Seen it all before, Larry?

Anger over her annual £115,000 PM payout

A cruel person might remind the Daily Mail of its September 24 headline 'At last! A true Tory budget'.

The resignation package is completed with a leader in which Tories are yet again 'drinking in the last-chance saloon'. Remarking that Truss was in office for less time than it took her to campaign for the job, the paper says that it had held high hopes for her:

> *For almost a decade, Miss Truss had a strong and demonstrable record in a string of Cabinet posts. Sadly though, in Downing Street she was hopelessly out of her depth.*
>
> *Incompetence, unforced errors, self-delusion, untethered ambition and hubris... that lethal combination meant she'd barely got her feet under the desk before she was turfed back out of the famous black door....*
>
> *In her resignation address outside No 10, there was little in the way of an apology for turning the party of Churchill and Thatcher into a*

laughing stock - and, worse, for making a Labour landslide at the next election a terrifyingly real prospect.

And her bleak legacy doesn't end there.

In a carefully orchestrated coup, the anti-Boris, anti-Truss faction - mostly Remainers - within the party have installed their men as Chancellor and Home Secretary.

FIGHT FOR SOUL OF THE TORIES

Naivety, dogma and haste, her fatal flaws

IN PICTURES, THE SHORTEST AND MOST TURBULENT PREMIERSHIP IN OUR HISTORY

Unleashing a radical agenda on a brittle and febrile economy sealed PM's fate

COMMENTARY by Daniel Johnson

'American-style libertarianism'

On this, the leader writers have reached the same conclusion as Littlejohn, but the paper has offered no evidence of any coup having been orchestrated – carefully or otherwise. The only person it had previously openly accused of plotting against Truss was arch-Brexiteer Michael Gove.

The editorial goes on to repeat the Mail's regret that Tory MPs ousted Boris Johnson 'over a cake', and says that if he could be 'persuaded' to run, it would send a shiver down Starmer's spine. It also lists Sunak and Ben Wallace as 'admirable' potential candidates and concludes that the party must take this last chance to pick a 'proven winner'.

Who could it possibly mean?

22 October

Scrummy new *Great British Bake Off* recipes
INSIDE WEEKEND MAGAZINE

Daily Mail

SATURDAY, OCTOBER 22, 2022 Daily newspaper of the year £1.30 90p to subscribers*

FREE HOME DELIVERY* FOR 13 WEEKS SAVE UP TO £45 SEE PAGE TWO

PLUS 30% OFF THE PRICE OF YOUR DAILY MAIL

As ex-PM and former Chancellor both see a surge in support and senior figures try to broker a deal, the tantalising question...

COULD BORIS AND RISHI NOW UNITE TO SAVE TORIES?

By Jason Groves Political Editor

SENIOR Tories are trying to broker a face-to-face meeting between Boris Johnson and Rishi Sunak in a bid to end the bloodletting engulfing the party.

Mr Johnson is understood to be willing to meet his estranged former chancellor in the hope of burying the hatchet and thrashing out a deal to govern together.

With the battle to succeed Liz Truss fast becoming a two-horse race, a deal between the pair could end the contest immediately.

Turn to Page 4

COMMENT

TORY MPs must wake up and face the brutal reality. Whoever wins the leadership election, the whole party must coalesce around them. The time for egos and petty feuding is over.

SEE PAGE 13

Having another shot: Former PM Boris Johnson

Bookies' favourite: Former chancellor Rishi Sunak

Johnson is heading home from the Dominican Republic and the Mail is dreaming of a Boris-Rishi double act. Pollster Matthew Goodwin writes on page 4 that for the sake of the country, the old team must get back together. But the final paragraphs of the splash concede that it is difficult to see how it would work. Sunak would be unlikely to return to the role he quit in July under Johnson, who would in turn not consider even a senior job, such as home secretary, in a Sunak administration.

FIGHT FOR SOUL OF THE TORIES

Now Tory big beasts line up to back Boris

Ex-PM sees dramatic surge in support with six Cabinet ministers leading clamour for a comeback

ON HIS CARIBBEAN HOLIDAY

Warm words from Ukraine

THE CABINET MINISTERS SINGING HIS PRAISES

But BoJo-blockers threaten to quit if he returns

AND HERE, TWO POWERFUL PARTY VOICES MAKE CASE FOR HIS RETURN

Party members are no fools. They know a winner when they see one

By Lord Cruddas

We need him. He's the standout political star of his generation

By Chris Heaton-Harris

FIGHT FOR SOUL OF THE TORIES

Tory MPs must move to axe Partygate probe if Boris returns, say allies

Scan this QR code to vote for who should be next PM on The Mail+

Q&A by Harriet Line

Now Javid backs Rishi as supporters push for a 'coronation' on Monday

Labour take 39-point lead in polls

The first of three spreads has the 'big beasts backing Boris'. These include Jacob Rees-Mogg and other household names such as Anne-Marie Trevelyan and Simon Clarke. Another of them, Northern Ireland Secretary Chris Heaton Harris, has a piece alongside explaining why – 'he's a winner'

– as does the Johnson-ennobled Lord Cruddas – 'he's the standout politician of his generation'.

Then it's Rishi's turn, as his supporters call for a coronation on Monday with no members' vote. But the left-hand side of this spread is also Boris-oriented, with further calls for the Partygate inquiry to be halted. There is also a sobering little story: Labour are now 39 points ahead in the polls.

Finally, the focus turns to Penny Mordaunt, the only declared candidate so far, and a new warning about her 'woke views' and a panel asking 'Is this really the right CV for a potential PM?'

Mordaunt's chances are dismissed - too woke, too inexperienced, poor work ethic - in a full-page leader running through the three most likely candidates. But the paper hedges its bets on the other two, whose careers were 'forged in the fire of Covid' and who had saved thousands of lives, livelihoods and businesses:

In all the cacophony over Downing Street parties and a birthday cake that never came out of its Tupperware box, the huge debt owed to both men is often forgotten.

Mr Johnson was elected with a landslide majority. It may be argued that he still carries that popular mandate. He made many mistakes...but the Mail believes a series of political molehills were heaped together and fabricated into a mountain by his many enemies to force him out.

Mr Sunak...has been proved right about the dangers of Trussonomics (though we still believe that with better execution, her tax-cutting agenda would have stimulated growth).

He did show a tendency to be thin-skinned during the leadership election and was less than wholly open about his wife's non-dom tax status. But he has certainly shown himself to be a politician of substance.

There were tantalising indications last night of a rapprochement between these two 'big beasts'. They were friends and solid political allies until Mr Sunak wielded the knife, Brutus-like, against his boss with his carefully choreographed resignation.

Let's hope they can again find common cause. A Johnson/Sunak ticket could be a potent force both internally and at the next General Election. It would surely steady the Tory horses.

Readers playing Mail Leader Bingo could tick off the Tupperware box, the Brutus-like assassination, but not the last-chance saloon. The editorial did, however, call on Tory MPs to 'coalesce' around a candidate.

24 October

Daily Mail

MONDAY, OCTOBER 24, 2022 Daily newspaper of the year 90p 55p to subscribers*

INSPIRE MAGAZINE STARTS PAGE 31

TORY LEADERSHIP SENSATION

Sunak firmly on course to become new PM after Johnson dramatically steps aside, saying: I had the numbers but it's simply 'not the right time'

RISHI SET FOR No10 AS BORIS BOWS OUT

Support: Rishi Sunak yesterday

Decision: Boris Johnson

By Harriet Line
Deputy Political Editor

RISHI Sunak was on course to be Britain's new prime minister last night after Boris Johnson dramatically pulled out of the Tory leadership race.

After a weekend of twists and turns, Mr Johnson released a statement saying he had 'sadly come to the conclusion' that it would not be right to stand. The former prime minister insisted he had the backers to make the ballot paper and could win a vote among party members. But he said this would 'simply not be the right thing to do'.

With Mr Sunak expected to win the support of the majority of Conservative MPs, Mr Johnson said he could not govern effectively without a united party in Parliament.

His decision means Mr Sunak is highly likely to become Britain's new prime minister today. The only other

Turn to Page 4

COMMENT

FOR the good of the party and the country, Mr Johnson set his dream aside. This is a gesture of wisdom, honour and statesmanship. His time will come again.

TURN TO PAGE 16

After marching his troops up the hill, Johnson marches them down again and says that he has decided not to stand after all. Even though he 'had the numbers' and thought he would win the members' vote and go on to deliver a 2024 election victory.

RISHI SET FOR No10

Boris: I had the numbers... but you can't govern without party unity

Will Rishi now get dragged into party probe witch-hunt?

For the Mail, this is 'a gesture of wisdom, honour and statesmanship'. But for Johnson it was perhaps more a confrontation with reality. He had, political editor Jason Groves reports, held talks with both Sunak and Mordaunt; both had rebuffed him.

He had therefore concluded that he couldn't unite the parliamentary party and govern effectively. This story also mentions a poll for the Mail's Sunday sister that shows Johnson would have been the most popular of the three potential leaders with the public – but that even he would have been expected to lose the next election to Starmer.

But all that is history, pushed back in the book. Sunak is the man of the moment and for once he is given precedence over his old boss, with the first spread – and the full-depth 'star-of-the-moment' picture slot reserved for Truss during the previous leadership campaign.

Here he claims that he can unite the Tory tribes, while home secretary Grant Shapps – the man denounced in a leader last week as a Remain-voting centrist technocrat – is given space for a bylined piece saying Sunak will stabilise the economy.

In the main story, Suella Braverman swings behind Sunak, having written in the Telegraph that Johnson had been the right leader at the right time, but that it would be naïve to look back on those days with sentimentality.

Within days, Shapps would be demoted and Braverman would be back in her old job.

RISHI SET FOR No10

Rishi: Now I will unite Tory tribes

Ex-Chancellor all but certain to be crowned as he pledges to work 'day in day out' to fix economy

'We can't deliver in deadlock'

'Clear plan to fix biggest problems'

By Grant Shapps

Sunak CAN put country back on track

The force is strong: Star Wars fan likely to be our next PM

Andrew Pierce reporting

Suddenly the columnists are all aboard the good ship Rishi. Stephen Glover brings out the word of the month to celebrate the fact that Britain is poised to get what it needs – 'a leader around whom warring Tory factions can settle and coalesce'. He had looked at the pictures of Johnson over the weekend and thought 'No thank you. Not now.'

Dominic Lawson says 'the Tory faithful may prefer Boris – but Rishi is the real rightwinger'. This on the page where many a leader had previously insisted that there must be a candidate from the Right – preferably Truss – to challenge Sunak and give party members a 'real' choice. Johnson, of course, was never of the Right. But he was a Brexiteer and a 'winner' and that was what mattered to the Mail.

Braverman might have cautioned against looking back at the Johnson era with misty eyes, but the leader is still wistful as it considers 'a remarkable act of magnanimity from perhaps the most brilliant politician of his generation'. Combining ruefulness with a swipe at Sunak's supporters and a warning for the heir apparent, it continues:

> *With his formidable campaigning skills, optimism and vision, and ability to woo parts of the electorate that had never voted Tory before - to great success in the Red Wall - who would have bet against him? For the good of the party and the nation he set his dream aside. This was a gesture of wisdom and statesmanship. By withdrawing from the race, he has spared his party a bloody and fatal civil war.*
>
> *Instead, he has placed a high value on loyalty, unity and discipline - the key weapons needed to keep Labour from getting their hands on the levers of power.*
>
> *Mr Johnson's generosity stands in stark contrast with the petulance of some of Rishi's supporters, who undermined Liz Truss out of spite after she won the last Tory leadership contest last month.*
>
> *Mr Sunak should not forget that he has ridden into power on Boris's coat tails.*

25 October

AFTER WEEKS OF TURMOIL, TORY PARTY FIGHTBACK STARTS HERE

Daily Mail

TUESDAY, OCTOBER 25, 2022 | Daily newspaper of the year | 90p | 55p to subscribers*

A new dawn for Britain

Rishi Sunak becomes our youngest modern PM – and first with an Asian heritage

THE FINEST ANALYSIS, COMMENT & REPORTING SEE PAGES 2-11

Sunak is elected unopposed and the Mail kicks off eleven pages of news coverage with a poster front page heralding 'a new dawn for Britain' and a red tab saying 'Tory fightback starts here' – which is exactly what the leading article said when Truss was elected on September 5.

RISHI'S NEW DAWN FOR BRITAIN

FAMILY BUSINESS

YORKSHIRE HOME

His grandparents came here with next to nothing. But hard work and education changed everything

Inspirational rise that torpedoes the Left's myth that Britain is a racist backwater

By Guy Adams

'My parents really struggled to put me through Winchester'

'OCD approach to loading the dishwasher'

MEET THE IN-LAWS

WEDDING CELEBRATIONS

RISHI'S DISHES

The tone is optimistic – there's an essay by Guy Adams on how Sunak's 'inspirational rise torpedoes the Left's myth that Britain is a racist backwater'. The piece is illustrated with the same boyhood picture of Rishi that was used alongside the 'Tory traitors' splash after Johnson's resignation in July. And there's still a hankering for Boris, with his allies insisting his day will come again.

A full-page leader characterises the former prime minister as gracious, honourable and statesmanlike, sacrificing his own ambition for the good of his party and the nation. Sunak is again reminded that he owes his new position to Johnson and that 'some will find it hard to forgive him wielding the knife against his former boss'.

But where he was previously the man who 'shamefully took the tax burden to a 70-year high', he is now 'unquestionably a politician of substance':

Mr Sunak mustn't learn the wrong lesson of the Truss debacle. The Tories are nothing if they're not a low-tax party

Daily Mail
COMMENT

His mettle was severely tested during the unprecedented Covid crisis – and he came through with flying colours.

As chancellor, he saved countless thousands of businesses and jobs with effective and imaginative support schemes.

An original Brexiteer, he has a ferocious intellect and understands the complexities of high finance and the global marketplace, making him a sound choice for these turbulent times.

And he is a man of considerable charm, a quality he will need in abundance to steady Conservative nerves and bring the party together. These diplomatic skills will also serve him well on the world stage.

Momentously, he also becomes the first non-white Prime Minister of this country. Not because of quotas or any obsession with positive discrimination, but entirely on merit. His elevation is a tribute to the Tories as the true party of diversity.

26 October

Daily Mail

WEDNESDAY, OCTOBER 26, 2022 Daily newspaper of the year 90p 55p to subscribers*

Who's in and out... Rishi's big reshuffle PAGES 6-14

Leave it to me, Your Majesty!

RISHI Sunak selected a unity Cabinet last night as he pledged to 'fix the mistakes' made by Liz Truss.

By Jason Groves
Political Editor

Following his appointment by the King at Buckingham Palace yesterday, the new Prime Minister removed 11 of his predecessor's Cabinet ministers in a frenzied hour of sacking, with Jacob Rees-Mogg and Tory chairman Sir Jake Berry among the casualties.

In their place he reinstated experienced former ministers such as Michael Gove, Dominic Raab and Steve Barclay, who returns as Health Secretary after being sacked from the same role by Miss Truss last month.

And, in an eye-catching move, Mr Sunak reappointed Suella Braverman to the post of Home Secretary just six days after she was fired for breaking the ministerial code by sharing a sensitive government document with a Tory MP.

The decision appeared to be a reward for Mrs Braverman coming out in support of Mr Sunak's leadership bid at the weekend, giving him crucial support from the Tory Right as he battled to head off a challenge

Turn to Page 4

Truss and her family are out. After the formal kissing of hands at the Palace, Sunak is installed in Downing Street, promising to 'fix' Britain with compassion.

The Mail approves of the new cabinet, especially the reinstatement of Braverman, comparing 'smiling Suella' with 'peeved Penny' after Mordaunt was denied the promotion she apparently sought. Much play is made in the ten inside pages of loyalty and the need for politicians to put party and country before self and personal ambition.

RISHI'S NEW DAWN FOR BRITAIN

Smiling Suella, peeved Penny – pictures that say everything

Braverman returns as Home Secretary six days after being sacked ++ But was Mordaunt snubbed for top Cabinet job... or did she simply turn it down?

LOYAL BACKERS (AND A FEW SURPRISES) IN PM'S TOP TEAM

Very brave, PM! Gove's back again

After six weeks of chaos, for which the Mail was at least in part responsible but for which it offers not an ounce of contrition, the relief in the leader is palpable. Sunak was 'statesmanlike and eloquent':

> *With Labour 37 points ahead in the polls and increasingly seen by voters as more competent on every issue, he exuded an urgency and sense of purpose that has been sorely lacking in recent months.*
>
> *You could almost hear the collective sigh of relief that the madness which has engulfed the Government may finally be over. The calm after the storm - we hope...*
>
> *Labour is calling for an election, but that is the last thing Britain needs in these parlous days (and they never complained when Gordon Brown was gifted power).*

As Mr Sunak said yesterday, this government has a clear mandate after winning a landslide in 2019 and its manifesto pledges have not changed...

Mr Sunak's grandparents came to Britain with nothing. The exalted position he now holds is down to hard work and education. To most people, he is an inspiration.

This is the man whose economic strategy as chancellor was vehemently opposed at every turn by the Mail, the man whose progress it did its utmost to halt, repeatedly saying he might never be forgiven for wielding the knife that felled Johnson.

This from the paper that urged Tory members to install Truss in No 10, a successful campaign that led to an unmitigated disaster that the paper blamed on everyone but her almost to the very end.

RISHI'S NEW DAWN FOR BRITAIN

I will fix Britain with compassion

Sunak vows to sort out Truss 'mistakes' while warning of 'difficult decisions' as he enters No 10

What he said... what he meant

Another day – and another lectern in Downing Street

When it was apparent to just about everyone in this country and abroad that her position was untenable, it said that party members would not stand for a 'coronation', that the public would not wear another unelected prime minister. Calls for a general election would be irresistible should she be toppled. Well, Sunak was installed unopposed and a general election is off the agenda – 'the last thing Britain needs'.

And now, no matter how often it feels the need to put the new PM right, the Mail will spend the next two years telling readers that – when they are finally allowed into the polling station – they must vote for him and not 'Captain Crasheroonie Snoozefest'.

Because he would crash the economy.

Postscript

That October 26 editorial says Sunak has a clear mandate to govern on the manifesto that gave the Tories their 2019 landslide. Even while Johnson was in office, the paper opposed the 'social levy' increase in national insurance, accusing Sunak of breaking 'a solemn manifesto commitment' by introducing it.

That manifesto also committed the government to a moratorium on fracking. The ban was lifted by Truss and immediately reinstated when Sunak came to office. On October 27 – the very day after saying the Tories' manifesto pledges had not changed – the Mail leader column carried this item:

Absurd fracking ban

With an energy crisis caused by a shortage of gas taking a wrecking ball to household budgets, it's absurd for Mr Sunak to ban fracking. He vowed to govern in the national interest, not kowtow to NIMBYs and the shrill eco-lobby for political expediency. Refusing to explore shale gas extraction means the PM is turning his back on a potentially transformative supply of low-cost energy, job creation and huge investment. Worse, he risks sacrificing our energy security, leaving us at the mercy of global market shocks and the belligerent whim of tyrants such as Vladimir Putin. It's truly contemptible for politicians to oppose fracking, while shedding crocodile tears over soaring gas and electricity bills.

Super-Postscript

The British Journalism Awards were set up to celebrate revelatory journalism on matters of public interest. They are open to anyone in any medium – local, national or international – whose work is published in the UK and are judged by a panel of some 70 experienced, and often distinguished, industry figures. Serious stuff.

At the awards dinner on December 15, 2022, the Guardian's Pippa Crerar scored a hat-trick, including taking home the top prize of Journalist of the Year. For breaking the Partygate story when she was the Mirror's political editor.

The industry clearly thought it mattered.

The category for which I was one of the judges was won by a writer from the Daily Mail.

Liz Gerard,

December, 2022

Bite-Sized Books

Why not sign up to our mailing list here:

Why not browse our BOOKSHOP?

Find out more about Bite-Sized Books here: